D1176232

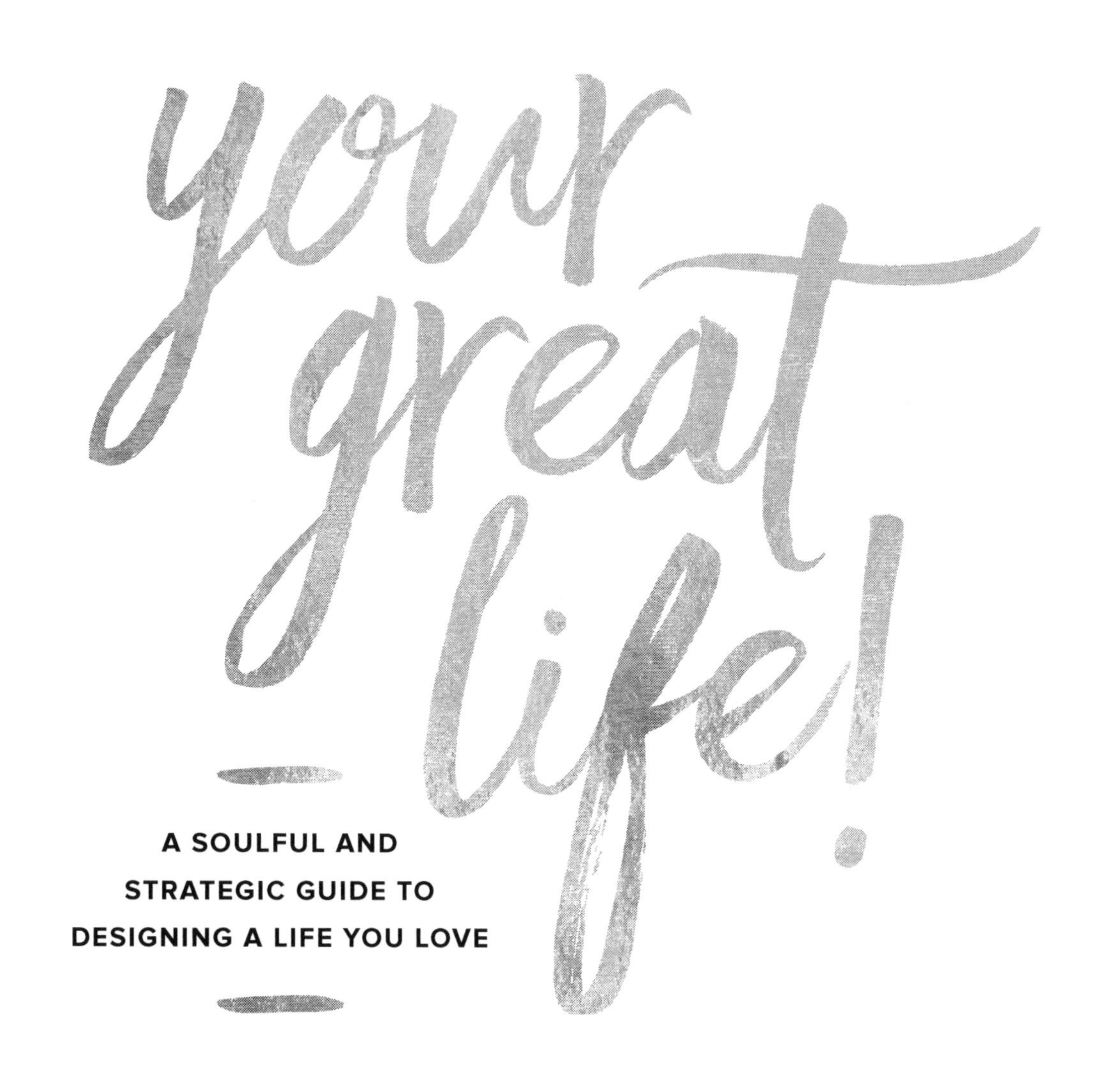

A SOULFUL AND
STRATEGIC GUIDE TO
DESIGNING A LIFE YOU LOVE

GEMMA STONE

live a life you love

add love to the world

GREAT LIFE CREED

LIVE BY THE GUIDANCE OF YOUR TRUE SELF.
When your life reflects the essence of who you are, you move in the direction of living a life you love.

YOU ARE MULTIDIMENSIONAL.
You are not just the bright and beautiful parts; you are also the dark and difficult parts. Knowing and loving all your bits creates space for living an authentic and aligned life.

LOVE MATTERS.
Design your life on a foundation of love. Choose love over fear, repeatedly. Life is too short not to love freely, fully and deeply. Our world needs your love.

NOURISH YOUR SOUL.
Listen to the desires, longings, and cravings of your soul. Fill your life with things, people, and opportunities that nourish your soul.

AUTHENTICITY IS ATTRACTIVE.
Knowing your true self and expressing it in the world will attract people and opportunities to support you in designing a life you love.

YOU HAVE WHAT YOU NEED WITHIN YOU.
Life design is not dependent on time, money, energy, age, approval, accolades, education, or anything else outside of yourself. You have everything you need to begin the life design process today.

DO YOUR INNER WORK.
Doing your inner work allows your outer world to evolve. Your mental maps will define and design the terrain of your life. Make sure they are accurate.

RESPECT YOUR INDIVIDUALITY.
People are like snowflakes – beautiful because of the diversity in the details. Celebrate your unique self and the distinctive life you will live.

COMMUNITY IS ESSENTIAL.
Find where you belong. Your tribe is waiting for you. You are not alone.

DO WHAT DEEPLY MATTERS.
Find the people and places that help you expand. Reflect frequently on this question: what matters deeply to me? Build your life around your core values.

YOU HAVE PERMISSION TO CHANGE YOUR MIND.
Who you are now is different from who you were then. What works for you today may not work for you tomorrow. You are free to change.

LIVE BY YOUR SACRED YES AND HONORING NO.
Be generous, but don't sacrifice yourself. Know your boundaries and honor them. Know your limits and transcend them. Serve others, support others, but don't live for others.

MAKE THE CALL.
In each moment you have a choice. Will you choose the life you love, or something else? Be conscious, courageous, and intentional. You are the designer of your life.

LET IT BE EASY.
But, it won't always be easy. Opt out of drama and trust yourself to navigate the difficult moments.

THE TIME IS NOW.
It's never too late. No matter how long you've been in the relationship, career, location, or mindset, it is never too late. We all arrive on this planet with possibility, potential and a desire to live a life we love. You haven't missed your chance. Now is the time.

CONTENTS

3

PART THREE – LIVE **240**

A MAP OF THE SACRED ADVENTURE

1

PART ONE – PREPARE

In part one, we will cover what you need to know in order to build a solid foundation for your life design adventure. We explore love, fear, true self, constructed self, ego, soul, life design values, and how to navigate this book. I know soul can be a confusing term. In chapter three, we're going to clarify what it means and why it matters for life design. By the end of this section, I hope you'll know that designing a life you love is worthwhile and do-able.

2

PART TWO – DESIGN

In part two, you'll warm up your creative muscles and expand your cognitive processes as you create the blueprints for living a life you love. This is where we dive deep into the life design process. We'll reflect on what you want in your life and what you need to release in order to make it happen.

3

PART THREE – LIVE

In part three, we will move your life design from creative concept into rocking reality. Here you'll craft your annual soul plan, establish rituals and commit to plans. We will connect with love and logic to strategically design your life.

PART ONE

PREPARE

It's better to look ahead and prepare, than to look back and regret.

JACKIE JOYNER-KERSEE

CHAPTER ONE

A LOVE LETTER, TO YOU

The frankest and freest and privatest product of the human mind and heart is a love letter.

MARK TWAIN

I KNOW YOU HAVE A SECRET DREAM, A LONGING, AN ACHING. SOMETHING PULLS at you, something brighter, bolder, more precious, more real, much more ... you.

That something is the life you love. I call it your great life. Great lives are not super lives; they are truthful lives. Great lives are not without tears and heartbreak, uncertainty and confusion. They are not lived for approval, applause, or accolades.

Great lives are born when you listen to the call of your soul. They are built from truth, integrity, courage, self-awareness, and vulnerability.

Your great life may involve a huge change – a move, a relationship transition, an adventure, a creative dream. Or, maybe it just needs a few small tweaks. Living your great life may mean your old world needs to die so your new world can be born. It may also mean having a difficult conversation, forgiving yourself, or becoming liberated from an old fear. Your great life may ask you to love yourself so completely and unconditionally that your heart breaks open. That wouldn't be such a terrible thing, would it?

When you hear your soul calling, you may be tempted to glance over your shoulder to see how your friends, family, culture, and society feel about the path you're being called to. They may be worried or confused; be gentle with them.

Life design isn't always easy or effortless – though sometimes it can be. You may have hesitations, doubts and uncertainties, or you may step into your great life with bold enthusiasm. No matter what, every step you take in the direction of a fuller, truer life brings you closer to what deeply matters.

Be prepared. Your ego will almost certainly protest your new life. You may hear the fears of your constructed self say, *who do you think you are?* You can respond lovingly with, *I'm my true self.* Suddenly, it's time to let the old habits and patterns of your constructed self crumble away.

When you choose to live the great life your soul is calling for, you may notice some fears rising.

What if ...

... I make a public declaration and I fall short?

... My friends and family don't understand?

... I don't like waiting in the unknown?

... I outgrow the people in my life?

... I make the wrong choice?

... I succeed?

... I fail?

... I transform my life in such a revolutionary way that the people I love no longer recognize me?

... I make the move, hand in my resignation, open my heart, take the leap – and instantly regret it?

... I spend heaps of time, energy, money, and effort chasing the dream that calls to me, only to end up back where I started?

... I start living my fuller, truer new life but long for my comfortable, familiar old routine?

I wish I could promise you these fears will never see the light of day. I wish I could guarantee you will be safe from discomfort. I wish I could support you by saying *every step of the journey will be easy.* I wish I could assure you that your loved ones will support and understand you. I wish I could comfort you with the knowledge your choices won't hurt anyone. I wish I could claim with absolute certainty that you will experience success with every decision you make and every action you take.

I really wish.

However, life design is subject to the realness of life. At least one of your fears may come true. But, it is just as likely the reality won't be as shattering as you expect. As you embark upon living a life you love, please remember, fear has a tendency to inflate itself. It likes to puff up into a sharp and prickly ball to scare you into staying stuck. Even if your fears do materialize exactly as you imagine, it won't necessarily mean you'll regret designing a life you love.

The whispers of your soul are meaningful and trustworthy. You are much more likely to regret ignoring them than to be sorry for heeding their call. As you follow your own advice, you will see the truth of your soul and the truth of your life. Trust it.

Please remember, there will be struggles in life no matter which path you choose. People will tell you what is right and what is wrong regardless of whether or not you live life on your own terms. There will always be dissenters, critics, and walls erected by the status quo. These things are unavoidable, so you might as well choose to live a life you love.

As you pursue the truth of your life, you will bond your heart and soul to like-minded people. Your love of authenticity and living a meaningful, fulfilling life will tether you to others who are doing the same. You will feel kinship, connection, and belonging.

Living a great life begins with a choice and continues with a belief: *I choose my soul's calling over all others. I am capable. I can handle whatever life puts in front of me.*

Do not mistake a designed life for a self-indulgent life. Living a life you love is a gratifying by-product of repeatedly choosing to live with consciousness, courage, and community. It's what happens when you choose to listen to your soul and do what is necessary to make it the truth of your life.

My dear Life Designer, at the end of your life you will look back and know you picked the sacred adventure – you designed your life the way you wanted it to be. You lived truly and fully. When you reached the fork in the road, you picked the path that allowed you to feel proud of who you are and how you spent your time on earth.

When you reach the moment where you face the ultimate decision – the predictable, familiar, untrue choice versus the unpredictable, unknown, truthful choice – you may experience a nervous edge, a stomach full of butterflies, sweaty palms, a mind filled with uncertainty. Take the first step and know you are not alone. There are many others walking right beside you.

A CAUTION

Life design isn't for everyone. Many people are completely satisfied with the status quo and automatic living. If your comfort zone is ... comfortable and you have no desire to expand it, I lovingly suggest you close this book now.

The questions, reflections, and processes that follow may make you uncomfortable. You might feel challenged and you may question everything you thought you knew about yourself, your life, and the world.

I want to be sure you are entering into this process fully aware of the risks, because there are risks. Of course, life design also offers tremendous rewards, but those rewards are not for everyone.

Whether or not you continue past this point, I wish you a great life.

You're still here. Wonderful!

Life design is an adventure that requires preparation. Without adequate preparation, it's easy to be unpleasantly surprised or unnecessarily challenged by the experience. The next few chapters are all about preparation. As you read through them you may notice a sense of urgency building within you, like you're ready to design your life immediately. I can relate.

When I was 25, I decided I wanted to hike the West Coast Trail – a beautiful and challenging 47-mile rainforest hike. I had never done a multi-day hiking trip before, but I felt the urgency to do it, so I signed up anyway. I read a few blog posts, climbed a few hills, bought a backpack, and found myself at the trailhead a few weeks later. I was unprepared. It was the hardest, most painful, most exhausting thing I have ever done (which is saying a lot, considering I birthed both my babies at home, alone). My hiking adventure didn't have to be that way. With a little patience and preparation it could have been the empowering and exhilarating experience I had anticipated.

I encourage you, as you move through the next few chapters, to allow your excitement to build, while being patient about the preparation process. It's the best way to ensure you get the most from your life design experience.

USING THIS BOOK

You found me – and I found you – for a reason. I trust life brought us together for a purpose. I feel like I know you, even if I don't know you. I know you have a story. I know you've had moments of suffering. I'm guessing, at times, you scramble to feel happy and deep down inside you have a dream, even if you don't yet know what it is or how it looks. I know there have been moments in your life when you've been told who you should be and what you should do. I know, at times, you feel the burden of expectations pressing down on you. I know you crave truth, meaning and purpose. I know you want the freedom to follow your heart's desire and I know you want to live a life that makes you feel excited and energized.

LIFE DESIGN IS FOR EVERYONE

I am amazed at the range of people who show up to life design. New moms struggling with an identity crisis, young artists searching for an inner muse, burnt-out executives, spiritual masters seeking more soul, enthusiastic entrepreneurs, and folks on the brink of retirement.

Life designers are also people who are madly in love with their spouse, surfing the single life, exploring alternative lifestyles, and rebuilding after a devastating divorce.
Life designers have been uncomfortably broke, comfy in middle class, or living the million-dollar life.

Everyone wants to live a life they love.

INTENTION

My intention is to support you to find your truth and give you some tools to help you design a life you love. This book includes theory, woven with philosophy, intertwined with story, and topped with process. When you explore a life design process in this book, I encourage you to make it your own, and mold it so it fits the shape of your life.

You may find life design takes over your days – in a really good way. Perhaps you'll keep a journal beside your bed to track 2 am insights, you may excitedly pull over the car to scribble down new inspiration, or even share a revelation with your barista. Researching and planning your great life will fuel your excitement for living. Taking a risk will feel less risky and more empowering.

Beware, this is not *Ten Steps to Living a Life You Love*, because my way is not your way. There are countless people in the world, especially the self-help world, shouting about what you 'should' be doing. This book is not intended to be a 'should-ing' list. Just because something works for someone else doesn't mean it will work for you. And, just because it works for you today doesn't mean it will work for you tomorrow. Adjust as necessary.

GUIDEBOOK

Jane Austen says, *"we have all a better guide in ourselves, if we would attend to it, than any other person can be."* I agree. Your Great Life is intended to be a guidebook as you adventure into yourself and the truth of your life. I've been on a few wild, outer world adventures and the most important thing I packed was my *Lonely Planet* guidebook. These books contain treasures of wisdom from people who travelled before me; they've helped me out of a few jams and made each adventure much more enjoyable.

The interesting thing about a guidebook is that, at some point, you won't need it anymore. Now, when I explore the world, I leave my guidebooks at home. A good guidebook will help you to build your confidence, trust yourself, and know you can find your own way. I hope this book helps you to deepen your confidence in life design, trust your true self, and understand that you have everything you need within you to create the life you love.

Make this book yours. It's your guidebook, vision board, art journal, sounding board and trusted friend. Add color, draw in the margins, fold the pages, highlight passages, sketch symbols, tape quotes, circle words. Claim it and make your mark – it is yours.

EVOLUTION OF LIFE DESIGN

This book emerged in layers and pieces, words and thoughts, processes and questions. It was disjointed and disorganized. I was inconsistent with my writing practice and often withdrew from the work for months at a time. You may experience a similar process as you design a life you love. You may be laser focused and swift in your implementation or it may happen slowly and sporadically. There's no right way, but what I know for sure is that the life you love, loves you right back. Just like this book was waiting for me to write it, the life you love is waiting for you to live it.

In this book you will find perspectives, processes, and stories to help you design a life you love. I'll share pieces of my life design story and share the stories of other life designers. I don't ask you to agree with our experiences, but simply to reflect on your own. As I speak the truth of my life, it may help you to see the truth of yours and to know that you are not alone. There is so much to know and so much truth to discover. The direction my feet take and what speaks to my heart may not be right for you. I share my spark of truth to guide you through the dark, but not to tell you what to see.

Life design is a process and it is a tool. Processes are only helpful when you engage with them, and tools are only helpful if you use them. You will have to engage with the processes in order to benefit from them. Learning how to engage in processes and how to use tools can take time. You'll need to practice and be patient. If you commit to the processes and embrace the tools, you will find yourself designing a life you love.

This book contains plenty of questions for which there are no right answers. This is not an intelligence test or an aptitude exam. It's not a psychological assessment and I won't tell you how your personality traits make you perfect for a certain kind of life. There are many personality tests out there that will explain what motivates you, illuminate what attracts you, and draw attention to what depletes you. While helpful in some ways, psychological tests are limiting. They give you very little insight into the truth of who you are and what deeply matters to you. Only you can know that. This book was written to help you connect to the most important person in your life – your true self.

Life design is a creative, conscious, collaborative experience. I'll offer up ideas, thoughts, reflections and questions, and ask you to filter them through your own truth and wisdom. It's one part art, one part science, and wholly about soul. It's a deep dive into the fullness of who you are and the life you want to live.

AUTHENTICITY

Writing and researching this book allowed me to experience corners of my soul that were previously inaccessible. Becoming aware of the truth – we alone are responsible for our lives – was essential to my salvation. While this book is intended to add liberation and love to your life, it is not about transcending the human experience; it's about being in it – soulfully embodied, fully alive, and profoundly real.

I've read a ridiculous number of self-help books and eventually, I became suspicious of transformation conversations that bypassed the messiness of human experience. I made a commitment to myself to write as authentically as possible. After making that commitment, I found myself writing stories I didn't want to write, but needed to share in order to keep it real. I now understand that by sharing the messy stories of life, we come to know we are not alone.

Here's what I know for sure: when you live your great life, you automatically liberate others to do the same. When you shine your light, you add to the collective light in the world. When your life is guided by your soul, you tip our world in the direction of love. And, our world desperately needs your special brand of love.

QUALITY QUESTIONS

This book is focused on helping you develop self-awareness to know what works for you (and what doesn't) when it comes to designing a life you love. Self-awareness is born from quality questions and conscious reflection. Throughout this book, you'll find life design processes based on quality questions that are intended to spark conscious reflection.

Questions that are based in fear build stories that can imprison us, but questions that are based in love give us the freedom to truly live. Fear-based questions typically perpetuate suffering.

> *How can I get my partner to meet my needs? How can I get people to like me? How can I make it through the day? How can I find security? How can I avoid rejection? How can I do all that is expected of me?*

The more we seek answers to fear-based questions, the less secure we feel. I will offer you questions and I encourage you to examine your questions as you move into the design of your life.

Do your questions empower you to grow more fully into your true self, or do they keep you stuck and cause suffering? Are your questions based in love or fear? Are you asking what your soul wants you to ask, or are you recycling questions from your parents, partners, teachers, or coaches? Do the answers to your questions cause you to open up and expand or to close down and contract?

The questions we ask ourselves define the lives we live. *What life do you want to live? And, what questions will allow you to live it?* Ask these questions once and they will redirect your day. Ask these questions every day and they will redirect your life. Every question you answer is a gift to yourself. Be generous.

CONSCIOUS REFLECTION

In addition to quality questions, I will offer sentence stems to guide you into soulful self-reflection. Stream of consciousness writing is one of my favorite processes for connecting more deeply with myself and uncovering the nuggets of wisdom my true self wants me to know.

Sometimes truth is buried deep in our psyche. Sometimes truth is just below the surface and we must simply blow off the dust. Either way, stream of consciousness writing is an excellent way to find buried treasure. You will unearth knowing that will feel both surprising and familiar.

When using stream of consciousness writing as a tool for self-awareness, it's helpful to trust the answer that emerges first and write, write, write. Replicate your answers if needed. Ramble. Be uncensored. Heart-felt. Anything goes – big picture, specificity, single words, run-on sentences, eyes open, eyes closed. No analysis – we all know it creates paralysis. The impulsive response is usually the one that is most truthful. And, life designers are truth-seekers.

MAKE IT REAL

This book is not just about answering questions and reflecting on your life. It's also about making the ideal real. You will design of your life by engaging in thoughtful action and by having courageous conversations. A little deeper into the book, you will find life design processes that are more directive, with an actionable flavor. Reflection gets you started on the design process and action transforms your design into reality.

I'm guessing you've already attended motivational workshops, set goals, attempted meditation, committed to a gratitude practice, and tried to live mindfully, so this isn't a "let's focus on your breathing, be present and practice gratitude," kind of book. This also isn't about adopting a "just push through it," little-engine-that-could mentality. This isn't syrupy positive thinking. We will venture into your psyche so you can emerge carrying the truth of your soul and the courage to live a life you love.

Though there is a general sequence to life design, you are free to adventure through the pieces that are most attractive to you. Stay curious. Stay inspired. Take a nibble and move on to the next one or devour the whole section in one large bite.

The life design processes are an important part of the adventure. Using these questions and strategies, you will deepen self-awareness and strengthen the skills you need to shift into living a life you love.

Let me be crystal clear -- life design is work. You will have to do the work. It takes practice and patience. You must actively unfold the life you love. Your true self will show you the path. It's up to you to walk it.

I feel light and alive when I ...

I feel heavy and burdened when I ...

When I love my life I tend to feel ...

If I were giving myself advice about living a life I love,
I'd say ...

CREATE SPACE

Be sure to carve out time and space to move into life design in a way that feels right to you. You can tackle it sequentially or you can jump about. You can start with the easiest element or leap into the most challenging one. You choose.

You may block off a weekend to power through or you may find yourself returning to it month after month. You might choose to adventure solo, with a partner, or join one of the book clubs that are popping up all over the world. If you're partnering up for this adventure, remember to share your experiences and reflections with your travel buddy; tremendous clarity comes from being seen and heard by another human. If you're going at it solo, your traveling companions will be Truth and Courage.

However you choose to design your life, please make it sacred and meaningful. This is how I create sacred space for my life design time.

> I greet the morning two hours before my kids wake up, and I head downstairs. I pull out my meditation pillow, light a beeswax candle, sip some green juice, and sniff my essential oils. I play with a few different meditation practices, go outside for a quick walk, and take a few deep breaths of fresh air. I head back inside to write and reflect on how I am living my life. A couple hours later, I hear the pitter-patter of small feet and my sacred life design time is complete.

You should know my life wasn't always green juice and beeswax candles. There was a time when I was working four jobs and sharing a basement suite in order to make ends meet. During that time, creating space for myself meant listening to a soulful song while sitting on the bus commuting between jobs and scratching out a few reflections in my journal. There are times when life is nuts. I totally get it. This is why I don't want to give you a to-do list for creating sacred space. Only you know what works for you, given who you are and what is happening in your life right now. Regardless of how you choose to move through the material in this book, it's paramount to set your intention.

INTENTION

Before you begin a life design session, reflect on how you want to feel and your intention for the time. Do you want it to be playful and energizing? Soulful and gracious? Liberating and loving? Clarifying and comforting? You choose. Once you've decided how you want to feel, it's time to set an intention.

Your intention is a way to focus your attention. It will guide you gently as you move through this book. It can also be helpful to state your intention as a question. Notice what it feels like to say, *as I read this book I intend to be loving to myself and listen to my soul.* It is positive, but closed, and it kinda feels like a 'should.'

Now, notice how it feels to say, *as I read this book, I intend to ask, how can I be more loving to myself and listen to my soul?* It feels open, curious, expansive, and encouraging.

Form your intentions around your deepest longing. Write it down as a reminder while you move through the life design process. Once you've decided how you want to feel and you have set an intention to support it, self-compassion is the last foundational element to establish.

Going through this book, reflecting on your life, reading the stories of others, and engaging with the processes could be really easy. And, it could be really hard. It might make you breathe deeply with peace or breathe deeply with exasperation. You might feel sad, frustrated, empowered, or encouraged. There might be moments when you want to quit and moments when it seems like a breeze. Whatever comes up, let it come up – it's part of the adventure. Whatever happens, remember to hold yourself in love.

I'm going to create space to design my life by ...

My intention while moving through this book is ...

CHAPTER TWO

THE POWER OF STORY

Stories can conquer fear, you know.
They can make the heart bigger.

BEN OKRI

THROUGHOUT THIS BOOK, I WILL SHARE MANY STORIES. YOU WILL READ stories from my life and stories from other life designers.

When I share stories of myself, I have tried to remember the facts of the past as accurately as possible, but the insights came after I had lived through the crisis. During my awakening moment in the bathtub, which I will share with you later, I was a highly medicated, sugar-addicted, slightly drunken mess. I broke open in that moment, but truth, love and wisdom didn't fill in the cracks until much later.

Many other life designers have generously supported this book by sharing their stories. Some identifying information may be altered to protect the storyteller's confidentiality; however, the themes, life lessons, and aha moments have all been left intact. These stories are vulnerable, sometimes raw, and always require courage to share. Opening up the deepest and richest parts of life can be daunting, but each and every one of them did it, for you, for me, for our world. They are amazing human beings. People who are living their great lives and want to help you live yours, too. These people have blessed my life; may they also bless yours.

While the stories are intended to illuminate and inspire, there is a catch. Don't do what they did. Not necessarily. Your great life is your great life. No one else can live it the way you will live it and no one can tell you which path to take. This is your journey, but there are many people walking beside you. These stories are meant to serve as guiding lights and they can help you to find your way, but they do not tell you where to go or what to see. No two people are the same. No two lives are totally alike. Every life design is its own work of art. This is your life, design it the way you want it to be.

As I share my story and the stories of other life designers, you may end up thinking, *this stuff is easy for them*. While that may be true for some life designers, it certainly wasn't for me. In fact, I wrote this book because until several years ago, my life was really bad and I was a hot mess. Debt was climbing, weight was piling on, and every year I needed a higher dose of antidepressants just to stay on top of the symptoms. Happiness was a long way off and living a life I loved seemed impossible. I know what it's like to feel drained and overwhelmed every day. Feeling unworthy, fearful, and not good enough was my comfort zone. Slipping into self-sabotage and self-sacrifice was all too familiar to me. I redesigned my life because I was barely surviving.

MY STORY

I was born a sensitive soul with an early start on darkness and trauma. The pain of my life caused me to disconnect from my true self by the age of five. I quickly developed a people-pleasing, self-sacrificing, good-girl persona. My trauma taught me that speaking the truth and taking care of myself causes a chaotic crash of abandonment, instability, and disconnection.

Most of my life I was an adept chameleon, altering myself to suit my surroundings and the expectations of others. As a young adult, my past started to catch up to me and I self-medicated with wine, shopping, and ice cream. In addition, I used a handful of prescription medications to keep the depression, suicidal thoughts, anxiety, and panic attacks at bay. I also kept my life overflowing with commitments; I would do anything I could to distract myself from the darkness.

Of course, at the time, I wasn't conscious of any of this. The story I told to justify my life was so elaborate, I couldn't see through the complex web of lies. As the good little over-achiever, I started winning awards and acquiring titles – captain of the sports teams, president of the jazz band, most 'inspirational' awards, and the Canadian Ambassador for my college. As life continued, I exchanged titles for roles, waking up at five in the morning to run off to one job, finishing my shift and starting my second job, finishing my shift and starting my third job. And, if a few available moments slipped free, I had a fourth on-call job to fill in the gaps. I was avoiding the pain of my life by zipping through it. Perhaps if I kept running, the pain couldn't catch me?

The whispers of my true self were so repressed that I didn't hear them until I turned 25. On my birthday, I decided to celebrate with a decadent bubble bath. I drove around town and collected everything I needed in order to honor my special day – fresh roses, a bottle of champagne, a box of Godiva chocolates, bubble bath, and luxury candles. When I returned home, I displayed the roses, drizzled the bubble bath, popped the champagne, and poured myself a glass. I laid back to enjoy my gift to myself and I felt totally ... empty. I looked at my bathroom sink and saw bottles and bottles of prescription medications lined up in a row.

Up until my birthday, I had seen dozens of therapists and read hundreds of books. I had tried EMDR, DBT, CBT, EFT, ACT, and a whole bunch of other therapies that involve a mouthful of initials. I saw therapists who asked me to tell them how events made me feel, ones who gave me worksheets, another who gave me stacks of books, and even one who gave me strawberry marshmallows. I cried, imagined waterfalls, challenged my thoughts, punched pillows, and drew pictures.

In a desperate attempt to heal myself, I dove into university and graduate school to study psychology. Eventually, I became a registered psychologist. As a student of psychology, I devoted myself to mastering the therapeutic techniques that had once been used with me. I hoped that by gathering degrees and certificates, I might find a way out of my suffering and help others find their way out, too.

Prior to my 25th birthday I had numbed, distracted and medicated myself so completely that I was $100,000 in debt, 100 pounds overweight, and I had no idea who I was. I knew who others wanted me to be and I dutifully showed up as that. Until I didn't.

My birthday bubble bath was my awakening moment. I realized my life was built on a foundation of fear and I needed to tear it down. I wasn't living my life. The part of me that had been showing up wasn't my true self, it was all false – and I knew that if I had the courage to climb the mountain of truth, I would find my real life. All I had to do was keep climbing. And surviving.

Once I woke up to my reality, it took years of soul-searching and healing to arrive at a place of authenticity. Thankfully, along the way, I was able to find wise mentors – people who inspired me to ask better questions, seek more truthful answers, and who held me accountable when I wavered. Some mentors I hired and some graciously donated their time. In all cases, I will be forever grateful for the impact they have had on my life.

With the loving and patient guidance of my mentors, I found my health and my life. In the past I had used my mind to avoid looking into my heart and healing my soul. I knew I needed to trade mind therapy for heart therapy, and I knew I had get to know my true self. Using various therapeutic approaches and my soul's guidance, I slowly began to heal the wounds of my past.

My first healing steps found me in an over-spiritualized, superficial space. I traded my addiction to Ben & Jerry's Chunky Monkey for self-help books. I was so determined to heal myself, I committed to reading a book a week for 10 years. I practiced my affirmations, listened to spiritual audiobooks as I slept, and looked up every ailment in Louise Hay's book, *You Can Heal Your Life*. I became a spiritualized version of my false self. Even though it wasn't soulful, it was a step in the right direction. I was too afraid to enter the dark, so I became addicted to the light.

By ignoring the darkness, it stayed in me, buried and festering. True healing came in when I had the courage to edge into the darkness. In one particularly intense group session I cried – hard. I stood in a circle of 40 people and surrendered. I dropped my ego, let the tears flow and choked on my sobs. I had contained the pain for so long that my body had forgotten how to breathe. It was my first public experience of intense vulnerability.

I know I'm not alone in this kind of suffering. I know we all struggle at times. Some rare folks have an entirely peaceful and trauma-free childhood. The majority of us experience a few physical, emotional, mental, sexual, or spiritual dust-ups. It's beyond the scope of this book to support you in healing the past, but it is important. When revisiting the past, it's helpful to seek allies who can create a safe and sacred place for healing. If past traumas are preventing you from living a life you love, please reach out for professional support.

Once I healed the past, I focused my energy and attention on loving the present and envisioning a future that felt light and free. The life design processes, questions and content were born from designing a life I love and helping thousands of others do the same.

YOUR LOVE STORY

Life design is about how to live and be in the world. It's about authoring the story of the life you love. The pen is in your hand, your life is a love story, and you are the main character. What story will you write? Structure your story according to what you cherish most. What is that? Love, beauty, adventure, connection, commitment, impact?

Will the story of your life be epic or meandering? Will it be a story of blazing glory or subtle surrender? Your life is your masterpiece; let the light of your soul shine through.

YOUR PAST STORY

Clarify how you got here. We all have a story. The story of our past shows us where we've been, but it does not define where we are going. In every moment we are making a decision to design a life we love – or not.

When I was younger, I loved skiing. My mom would pack us up early every weekend morning and drive us to the hill. The slopes would open at 8 am and we'd be carving tracks until the lights went out. There's something sacred about being the first on the hill, floating through fresh powder. I would often look behind me, admiring how my skis sliced through the snow, analyzing my turns and noticing how I could improve. Then I would look forward, where the rest of the hill was open. I could go anywhere I wanted to go. The tracks behind me were beautiful and I was free to choose my next turn. There are many things I appreciate about my snow-loving days, but one lesson rises to the top: our tracks show us where we've been, but they do not determine where we are going.

The story of your life is powerful. Everyone has a story and every story is layered. Parts of your life have already been written, and while you can't change the facts, you can change your perception. How do you perceive your past? And, what perception would bring you more freedom in the present? The facts of the past are the facts, but your story of what they mean can change everything. If you're not interested in changing your perception of the past, focusing on writing a future you love.

YOUR FUTURE STORY

Living a life you love means honoring all of who you are. We all have the ability to design our lives to match our desires. Sometimes we get off course and end up with a life that feels draining. We feel hobbled and paralyzed, unable to detect the call of the life we love. So, we resort to what is comfy and familiar – our to-do lists, unhealthy coping mechanisms, busyness, old habits, and self-help books.

We all arrive on this planet with possibility and potential and a desire to live a great life. With all the demands we face and all the balls we juggle, our vision can veer off-course and even end up in the ditch.

The true you – the vibrant, alive, dynamic, creative, expressive parts of you – can be uncovered. Even if your constructed self feels broken or damaged, your true self is whole and complete. You have everything you need to design a life you love. Your confusion, your clarity, your light, your dark, your knowing, your questioning, your deviance, and your divine are all pathways on the sacred adventure of designing a life you love.

Showing up and brilliantly living your own unique part will complete the whole. When you fall in love with your life, you add to the love story of the cosmos. If we are to survive as a species, the collective story of our world must be a story of love. We need your love story in order to be complete.

My mother believed strongly in the power of gratitude. Every time my sister and I received a gift, she would immediately have us write a thank-you letter to the giver. Over the years, I began to find the act of writing letters inherently gratifying. When I traveled, I would write letters home. While commuting on the bus, I would write to my pen pal. When I was lonely, I would write letters to my friends. Once I became a psychologist, I began writing birthday cards and occasional letters to my clients. I rarely heard back from the clients I wrote to, yet I continued to write because I knew in my heart it mattered. One year, I received a phone call from a client who was struggling with depression. She had received my letter and read it every day for the entire year. "Your letter saved my life," she said. My mother taught us something that mattered to her – gratitude. I maintained my commitment to add to the love in the world by writing letters. Honoring our unique parts can save someone's life.

I've heard stories of how a stranger's smile helped a stressed-out mom to avoid yelling at her kids, how witnessing a courageous conversation with one person inspired a courageous conversation in another, how receiving a warm cup of coffee and an hour of conversation gave a homeless man the will to turn his life around, and how one kind adult in a troubled adolescent's life helped her to avoid trading sex for money.

How you choose to live your great life matters. As Dr. Martin Luther King Jr. said, "Everybody can be great… because anybody can serve. You don't have to have a college degree to serve. You don't have to make your subject and verb agree to serve. You only need a heart full of grace. A soul generated by love."

What do you really love about your life and why?

I want the story of my life to be ...

When I look at the past, the lesson that I keep trying to learn is ...

CHAPTER THREE

HELLO SOUL, GOODBYE EGO

All of us have a deep reservoir of mystical experience that sustains the part of what some call the soul. The soul yearns to be nourished, and if the reservoir begins to run low, we feel ourselves becoming dull, empty, brittle, and arid. If it sinks lower, we enter into states of angst, despair, and depression.

RABBI DAVID COOPER

THE MEANING OF PSYCHOLOGY IS 'THE SCIENCE OF THE SOUL.' THE GREEK word for soul is psyche, or what gives our life meaning beyond our physical body. The soul is also known as the true self. Throughout this book I will refer to the true self as a guide to designing your life that allows for authentic expression, a feeling of being fully alive, and living a meaningful life. Conversely, building your life from the constructed self leads to a life that feels fake, empty, and full of suffering. The constructed self is also known as the ego.

TRUE SELF

At its most foundational level, *Your Great Life* is about living from your true self over your constructed self. When we are born, we are fully connected to our true selves. As we live, we develop a constructed self in order to learn how to function in our world. Your true self doesn't change over time; you just become more skilled at tuning into it. Your soul is steady and your ability to see it, feel it, hear it, and know it will evolve through the life design process.

When you are living from your true self, you will recognize it by the qualities you experience in your life. Your true self feels secure, accepted, unconditionally loved, peaceful, and certain. When the world is chaotically swirling around you, your true self will remain stable and you will have a calm sense of knowing. The true self is connected to what deeply matters – it remains connected to meaning, purpose, and being of service. It is self-reliant, evolutionary, and creative. Living from your true self will build your life upon the solid foundation of truth and love.

CONSTRUCTED SELF

The constructed self emerges from a desire to get love, as in *maybe if I'm nice enough, smart enough, funny enough, obedient enough, rich enough, or pretty enough, they'll love me.* It is built to protect us from feeling weak, inadequate, overwhelmed, or vulnerable. When we are young, we astutely observe and meet the demands and expectations of others in order to be accepted, safe, and loved. The greater and more extensive the expectations, the thicker the mask of our constructed self becomes. Sometimes we mask our true self so effectively that even we can't find it anymore.

The constructed self is often overwhelmed by stress, crisis, scarcity, agitation, drama, doubt, fear, and insecurity. When you are swept away by outside influences, feeling lost, panicked, or confused, you know your constructed self is running the show. The constructed self will build a life from fear and insecurity.

For most people, the constructed self is largely unconscious and we don't even know it's there. When challenged to examine the constructed self, many people deny its existence; the constructed self can be tricky like that. The constructed self helps us to avoid repressed emotion and distracts us from unacknowledged pain. It dodges the light with compulsive storytelling, dramatic distractions, chronic cuteness, assuming intellectual superiority, thwarting with defensive retaliations, and stalling with insatiable busyness.

As we navigate through early life, developing a constructed self is a necessity. We develop a constructed self in order to understand our relationship to others, explore our place in the world, and experiment with the work we want to do. We all have a constructed self. The problem lies not in having a constructed self, but in mistaking the constructed self for the true self. We struggle and suffer when we identify with the constructed self over the true self. The constructed self stifles consciousness and authentic expression – and both are necessary in order to live a life you love. When we believe we are our constructed selves, we operate under a trance of mistaken identity. We lose our presence, live our lives on autopilot, and abandon what matters.

TRUE SELF VERSUS CONSTRUCTED SELF

I have noticed that when a client is living from their true self, they are more likely to experience peace, fulfillment, and energy. When they are living from their constructed self, they are more likely to experience turmoil, emptiness, and lethargy. I frequently see my clients' symptoms emerging in resistance to the life the constructed self has built. Depression, anxiety, procrastination, self-sabotage, and fear have many sources, but often they emerge from a suffering soul.

When our soul is suffering, we feel empty and we try to fill the gaping hole with anything we can find: ice cream, vodka, sex, Prada, Prozac, workaholism. We are seduced by anything that feeds us, yet we continue to starve.

When we feed our soul, we are satiated. We feel whole and complete. When we are in service of our soul, we feel energy and enthusiasm. Of course, energy can also come from a triple espresso or a rush of adrenaline. The key is to notice what provides sustained energy over time. Notice your feelings, level of satisfaction, and sense of meaning. If you are doing something that is not right for you, over time, you will feel your energy drain, unwanted symptoms will emerge, and your soul will retreat.

People often say, "I'm being true to myself," which is a very good thing. But, to which self are you being true? The constructed self can dig you deeper into suffering. The true self will guide you into a life you love. As you explore this book, you will become increasingly aware of the voice of the true self and the voice of the constructed self.

Freeing your life from the constructed self can seem daunting. We are scared to feel the pain underneath the coping strategy, we fear we might lose love, and we doubt our capacity to navigate the change. Removing the constructed self can feel vulnerable and shaky. It means dismantling defense mechanisms, redefining lifelong roles, and challenging ancient beliefs.

Returning to the true self requires self-discovery, not self-improvement. We are not trying to fix our constructed self or destroy our ego. Instead, we are focused on remembering our true self and identifying with our soul.

The work you do throughout this book will ripple into your life. You will separate ego from soul. What is unreal from what is real. And you will separate fear from love.

My constructed self is most likely to show up as ...

I can recognize my constructed self by ...

When I'm living according to my constructed self, I feel ...

WHAT IS SOUL?

Every soul is unique. The soul is the meeting place of spirit and body. It's both earthly and transcendent. It's the eternal essence of who we are. I've encountered many people on the healing path who skip over the soul and go straight to the spirit. When we skip the soul, our bodies and minds protest. We must come back down to earth and embody the soul if we are going to live a life we love.

Your connection to the Divine – God, Jesus, Shiva, Shakti, Creator, Allah, Gaea, Buddha, Mother Nature, Angels, Universe – is your spirit, whereas the soul is the observer in each of us. When we interact with the world, we receive light waves and sound waves. When we observe these waves, we change them. These waves become electrical impulses that the brain converts into images. Then, our consciousness observes those images and makes meaning from them. Our soul allows us to observe the world with individuality. Without the soul we would all experience the world in exactly the same way.

Our soul reports its satisfaction or dissatisfaction through our bodies, our emotions, and meaningful dreams. It is always guiding us to healing and wholeness. When we are disconnected from our soul, we tend to live in more anguish. We are more susceptible to unconscious living and we desperately scramble to regain the love we think we have lost. We slap Band-Aids onto wounds that can never heal without the wisdom of the soul. When you reconnect to the fire of the soul, the Band-Aids go up in smoke, the wounds are cauterized, and true healing begins.

Your soul will design a life based on what is nourishing and meaningful. It will design a life that is connected to the core of who you are and that reflects your values and sense of purpose. The soul designs your life based on personal truth and authenticity. The soul is fluid, flexible, and moves through life with ease. It sees the perfection in imperfection.

WHAT IS EGO?

The ego is another name for the constructed self. If you are not living with soulful presence, you will find yourself trapped in the prison of ego. A life designed by the ego is stressful, draining, and often leads to depression and anxiety.

Your ego will try to design your life based on what you *should* be doing, what it thinks a good person would do, or the parts of yourself it doesn't like and wants to fix. It will design a life based on outside expectations or in pursuit of approval and popularity. The ego is rigid, it will expect you to be perfect, and it will hassle you to achieve every goal you set for yourself. The ego typically seeks comfort and security. On the other hand, ego may rebel against social norms just for the sake of rebelling.

Helping the ego to step out of the way is essential. If we allow our egos to lead, we are vulnerable to unhappy, unhealthy, unfulfilled years. If we live this way for too long, a part of us dies. Though our bodies will continue walking through life, we will feel as though we are not truly alive.

When I first began moving into life design, my soul expressed a longing to have a bigger impact. I was terrified of public speaking at the time. I resisted it for a few years and then slowly, I let my soul take the lead. At one of my early speaking gigs at a wellness festival, I was asked to share what I knew about living from love over fear. When I was slated to get on stage, there were two people in the audience. Two people! Needless to say, fear kicked in something fierce. I was tempted to beeline out of there and spend the afternoon playing with my kids at the park.

My ego was especially nasty that day, taunting me with refrains of *you're not good enough. People don't want to hear what you have to say. And you should never, ever, ever take another speaking gig. Remember that woman who criticized you last year? She was totally right!* I was a paralyzed.

I tapped into my soul. It reminded me, *it doesn't matter how many people are there; speaking lights you up, and you might make a difference in one person's life. It's totally worth the risk of looking like a goof. Failure is progress, so even if it seems like you've failed, you're still moving in the direction of living a soulful life.* Deep breath. I invited the two people to sit with me at the front so we could have an intimate chat. Then something magical happened – others migrated over. By the end of the talk, I was smiling at dozens of people.

When you step in the direction your soul wants you to take, it might not work out as planned. But, when you step into your fear, you make space for magic and miracles. And whether magic and miracles happen or not, the greatest gift of all is the voice of your soul becoming a little stronger and a little louder.

LOVE OVER FEAR

This book was born from thousands of hours spent researching, a decade of personal journeying, and from helping thousands of clients to design their lives. The most important lesson I have learned in my life is to choose love over fear. Again and again. Love will be your primary motivating force when designing your life. Love. Not duty, obligations, expectations, fame, fortune, fear, guilt, shame, or blame. Love.

Pace Smith, a pathfinding coach, has the statement, *can love be found even here?* inked across her wrist. It is a reminder that love can be found in the darkest moments and in the most fearful situations. Pace could have tattooed the statement, *love is available even here,* on her wrist, but she knew she would be more likely to brush it off as a clichéd platitude. Phrasing it as a question instead of a statement encourages her to reflect with curiosity in her mind and sincerity in her heart. It's a powerful question. When faced with a difficult situation, ask yourself, *can love be found even here?*

The rules of love and fear are tangled in a hundred billion brain cells, amongst complicated electrical currents, and within a complex blend of hormones and neurotransmitters. Love emanates from the brain, but its reach extends further. Love and fear influence all human thoughts, feelings, and behaviors.

The world is full of people who struggle with living from fear instead of love. I was one of them and I have worked with many more. Living a life we love depends upon resolving the struggle between love and fear as quickly as possible. Whether we live in a state of love or a state of fear changes everything – love and fear make us who we are and create who we become.

Children who do not understand gravity fall while climbing and get hurt. Similarly, people who do not understand the principles of love spend their lives suffering. Dreams are abandoned, unhappiness becomes chronic, passions are neglected, anxiety soars, and depression settles in.

* * *

Noelle struggled with the fear of judgment. Her fear prevented her from speaking up in conversations and following her dream of being a writer. She would often set a goal for herself and quit before she was able to achieve it. At the life design retreat, Noelle processed and released the fear of judgment and stepped into being more loving and less fearful. When she returned back to her life, she noticed people began coming up to her and starting conversations. "Before letting go of this fear," says Noelle, "I would put off a vibe that kept people away because I was so afraid of being judged." In working through the fear, Noelle became more approachable, felt more connected to others, began writing the book she always wanted to write, spoke her truth in conversation, and has maintained her commitment to her soul plan. "Fear is a liar," says Noelle. "If you can move through it, it's awesome on the other side."

* * *

Choosing love over fear means living your life according to what you want to embrace, rather than what you are trying to avoid.

It means you focus on the good, practice gratitude, and trust life. Love will guide you to take the high road, while fear will drive you to control and manipulate. Love will ask you to be

Think about a challenging situation in your life.

Can love be found even here?

The messy fears that are interfering with the life I love are ...

If I was living my life from love over fear, I would ...

WHY LIFE DESIGN?

Why is life design worth it? Without life design, suffering engulfs us, confusion sucks time, inauthenticity feels gross, and unaligned decisions are costly. When you connect to your true self you can live more efficiently and effectively. You make better decisions, have healthier relationships, and are less likely to be derailed by mental health challenges. You will trust your choices, channel your energy, generate confidence, and build momentum. Living in a state of flow is a natural byproduct of designing a life you love.

Why must you answer the call to awaken your soul? Because, once you awaken, your soul will never let you go back to sleep. You will know that your time is precious, and you will no longer be content to sacrifice your time and energy on that which does not deeply matter.

Why must you answer the questions your soul asks? Because, you will see through the illusions your ego has created, you will discover how to unlock the chains that bind you, and you will have the courage to put yourself in the way of change.

Why must you remember the truth of your soul? Because, you will be liberated from superficial expectations, repetitive talk, limiting beliefs, and false labels. You will be guided into the adventure of knowing who you are now and who you are called to become. You will understand that knowing and trusting your soul is as necessary to life as breath and blood.

My relationship with my ego is ...

My relationship with my soul is ...

In what ways are you living a life you love?

In what ways are you not living a life you love?

What would it take for you to be utterly devoted to living a life you love?

MAGIC
POWER
OF
YOUR
MIND
YOU

CHAPTER FOUR

THE FOUR C'S OF LIFE DESIGN

Every child is an artist. The problem is how to remain an artist once he grows up.

PABLO PICASSO

CONSCIOUS REFLECTION CONTRIBUTES TO A STRONG SENSE OF SELF-WORTH and a clear understanding of the life your true self wants to live. Courageous action leads to authentic change and blossoming resilience. Having a community to support you in living a life you love is what makes life design sustainable. Creativity can help you connect to the three core values of life design: consciousness, courage and community.

CREATIVITY

Your Great Life is one part science and one part art. Life design is a creative cognitive endeavor. We want to sync up your left and right brain in new ways. Lighting up neural networks in unfamiliar patterns can help you tap into your truth, rather than the ancient thought pathways you've been taught to use. Life design is a magically creative and profoundly practical process. I will give you life design tips based on the psychology of change, and I will encourage you to express your insights creatively.

Creativity puts us in an altered state and allows us to dynamically explore what is possible. Life design is about exploring possibility, gaining clarity, and committing to aligned action. Express your thoughts, reflections, ideas, and desires creatively throughout this book. Creativity is a conduit for joy and self-awareness. Creative expression can enhance our capacity to solve problems, regulate emotions, increase adaptability, spark innovation, improve our immune systems, reduce boredom, and manage stress.

Creative expression also gives us a sense of balance and order. It makes hard things easier, strengthens integrity, boosts optimism, wards off loneliness, resolves conflict, and settles us into wellbeing.

Your relationships will also benefit from your creative expression, as creativity has been known to enhance empathy and deepen understanding. If we dive into the physical benefits, we see how creative expression improves health and longevity, reduces medication use, and increases activity.

The list goes on. Creativity makes us more conscious, observant, collaborative, dynamic, resilient, and brave. Compared to writing sentences, visual expression often leads to more insights and ideas. Sketch your relationship with your true self in the margins, and when designing your annual soul plan in chapter 11, create a visual representation. Visual journaling will spark different areas of your brain than word journaling alone can illuminate.

As you move through the questions in this book, ask yourself, how can I express this creatively? Find some inspiration by watching a child play, pick up some interesting supplies at your local scrapbooking store, write a poem about a concept that inspires you, or mind map your intentions and actions.

In this book, I will ask you to immerse yourself in the desires of your soul, feel your feelings, explore your experiences, expand your consciousness, and deepen your connection to yourself. Your great life is always calling, and creative expression can help you tune in and turn up the volume.

Creative life design is all about finding your own way. You will be invited to shine light on dark corners and you may be asked to choose the road less traveled. There's a chance your path does not exist, so you may need to create it as you walk it. I do not know the path you are meant to walk – nor does any other author, workshop leader, or guru. It's tempting to search for answers outside of yourself, and while outside answers may help to illuminate a path, it will not be your true path. Others can only know their path, just as only you can know yours. I never want you to follow me, or another, for you will end up lost. Creativity will lead you into the life you love.

How are you creative?

What tools or materials do you need to express your creativity throughout the life design process?

CONSCIOUSNESS

It is not until you awaken and become fully present that you will realize that you have not been present. It is not until you awaken that you will realize you have been asleep, dreaming that you are awake.

LEONARD JACOBSON

Throughout our lives we make choices. These choices become the design of our lives and the lives we live become the homes of our souls. In order to live soulful and meaningful lives, we must consciously and courageously choose how we live, love, parent, and work. There are an infinite number of options available in this wild and crazy world, and in order to fall deeply in love with our lives, it is imperative that we consciously choose the options that call to our soul.

Do you ever feel like you're drifting through life, wondering how you ended up where you are?

Are you working in a job you fell into?

Are you spending most of your time doing things you don't love doing?

Are you in relationships that don't feel aligned?

Is taking care of yourself last on your list of priorities?

Do you wake in the morning and dread another day of busy-work?

Do you feel like there's not enough time to do what matters?

Do you find yourself with an empty bank account at the end of the month and wonder where all your money went?

If you answered yes to a few of these questions, living consciously might bring you a whole lot more satisfaction and fulfillment.

Neale Donald Walsch says, “a life lived of choice is a life of conscious action. A life lived of chance is a life of unconscious creation.” Living consciously means examining the thoughts that bubble to the surface and questioning their validity, rather than assuming their accuracy. It means reflecting on why you do what you do, being honest about how it’s working for you, and changing course as necessary. It’s about designing the life you want, rather than settling for the one you have unconsciously stumbled into.

Cultivating a conscious lifestyle takes time. It’s a way of being in the world that grows stronger with practice. How do you live a conscious life? It’s deceptively simple. Think about what you are doing and how you are being. Be vigilant. Disengage autopilot. You are sovereign. You are the master of your domain. Reign consciously.

I often sit across from my clients and wonder, *if they were living a life they loved, how would they think, feel and act?* I find myself becoming a hybrid of Sherlock Holmes and Michelangelo – trying to uncover the clues and deduce where they lost themselves. We chip away at everything false so what is true can emerge, just as Michelangelo chipped away at the stone that kept David hidden.

Living a life you love means living in the realm of who you really are and why you are here. In order to know these two things, it is essential to commit to living a conscious life. The call to live a conscious life usually begins with a subtle stirring – an indiscernible whisper or a microscopic shift in perception. It’s the niggling sensation that it’s time for your work or relationship to shift. It can also be an internal poking, telling you that the unhealthy habit you’ve been wanting to eliminate will catch up to you really soon if something doesn’t change. Or perhaps it feels like a pull – to a new location, to relate to yourself in a new way, to have a difficult conversation, or to write the book you’ve always wanted to write.

If we trust those early signs, tune into them, and make the changes they suggest, we experience space and ease. If we ignore them for too long, the whispers become shouts and the stirrings become chaos.

Through habitual, unconscious and egoic living, we lose our sense of curiosity, it becomes difficult to know truth of the heart, and fear can more easily control the course of our life.

We all have an internal desire to move closer to our true self. When you embody your true self, you unleash an infinite capacity for creative and courageous change. By living a conscious life you are choosing to trust your true self over your constructed self.

We all want to feel full in our being, but when we live unconsciously, we become too full in our doing. We wander through life with a never-ending to-do list and we neglect our to-be list. One of the easiest ways to avoid consciousness is to distract ourselves with to-dos. And, let's be honest, distraction is the norm for many of us. We fill our ears with music when we're running in nature, we Instagram our morning meditation, we incessantly check our email, we text while we're driving, we work more so we can spend more so we can distract more. The moments of stillness are precious. It can be tempting to grab a book, open Facebook, call a friend, eat something, go shopping, or flip on the TV. If we allow it, our distractions can drown out what is sacred. It is all too easy to find ourselves living distracted, semi-conscious lives. It's easy to ignore the soul. Until it isn't.

Once you recognize that the disturbing dreams, draining tasks, empty relationships, body complaints, and mental fogginess can be the protests of a malnourished soul, these messages become very difficult to ignore. The remedy often begins with conscious reflection.

Life design starts with an inner journey of consciousness before it evolves into an outer journey of choice and change. There are times when my life design friends and I reference the 1999 film, The Matrix, and joke about which pill we took. The red pill represents choosing conscious living and the, sometimes painful, truth of reality. The blue pill represents the blissful ignorance of illusion and unconscious living. Will you go for the red pill or the blue pill?

The blue pill leaves us as we are, with unexamined habits and limiting perceptions. It allows us to continue to identify with the constructed self and to unconsciously conform to the expectations of others.

To take the red pill is to commit to asking quality questions, living mindfully, pursuing philosophical reflection, and exploring conscious reasoning. When you choose the sacred adventure of life design, you are choosing the red pill. In the beginning of my life design adventure, there were times I wished I had taken the blue pill, but now I know better.

I choose red.

How are you living consciously?

How are you living unconsciously?

Will you choose the red pill or the blue pill? Why?

If I was amping up my level of conscious living, I would ...

I'm going to cut a few things from my to-do list, including ...

COURAGE

Courage doesn't always roar. Sometimes courage is the little voice at the end of the day that says I'll try again tomorrow.

MARY ANNE RADMACHER

If we are to live our most authentic and meaningful life, we must choose courage over the fear-based call to do what is expected of us. A soulful life is a courageous life.

Designing a life you love is not always an easy task and it requires courage. I will ask you to be responsible for yourself and respond authentically. The life design process may be scattered with challenges and obstacles, but your soul has the strength, determination, resourcefulness, and resilience to deal with anything that comes your way. Your task is to trust it and surrender to it.

The first time I redesigned my life, it felt terrifying, healing, liberating, and painful. It was different than other breakdowns. In the past, I would respond to the hint of a breakdown with a bottle of wine, box of chocolates, and a new pair of shoes. I numbed and distracted until the threat of the breakdown passed. This time was different. I committed to feeling what I was feeling. I allowed myself to excavate the deepest parts of my psyche, to go into the dark and scary corners of my unconscious, and to call on all the courage I had to face the scariest thing I knew. My breakdown turned into a breakthrough.

RESPONSIBILITY AND REFLECTION

To live courageously, we must be responsible and reflective. If we don't enter into reflection and responsibility, we tend to seek comfort over greatness, safety over risk, reassurance over authenticity, the predictable over the unknown, and the well-worn path over forging our own. Reflection and responsibility do not lead to life balance or acceptance from others; they lead to greater freedom and authenticity.

Now is the time to take responsibility for yourself and your life. Cleanse yourself from blame; it's toxic and will poison your desire to be conscious and to live a life you love.

Releasing blame can be complicated, as it is often passed down through generations and cultures. Blame, and its cousin Shame, are used liberally to keep people in check and are often woven into our lives in such a profound way that choosing not to live with them can mean unraveling your life. Although it's a daunting task, it is a necessary one. Shame and blame are plagues that poison people, relationships, lives, communities, and countries.

When we remain hostage to the constructed self, we tend to cling to past shame, blame, grudges, injuries, and wounds. When we cling, we are inviting these states to darken our present like an unending eclipse of the sun. Living a life we love means healing the past and releasing it with love.

As children, we had to look to others for protection, guidance and care. Regardless of whether those needs were fulfilled, at some point, we have to grow up and become responsible for our own lives. If not, we will perpetually long for what was missing and become stagnant while waiting for others to give it to us. We must become responsible for ourselves and our lives.

The constructed self tells us that constantly revisiting past hurts will protect us from pain, but in reality, it prevents us from taking the risks that are required to live a life we love. To end the cycle, it is important to look inward and accept responsibility for what you find. Are you blaming others for the life you are living? We do not have control over other people in our life – not even the people we love the most. We do have control over how we choose to engage with others, our life, and the world.

* * *

When Leigha turned 40, she suddenly found herself the object of romantic attention from multiple men. While she enjoyed this attention, she felt conflicted because she was married. For six months, she negotiated her need and desire for attention, protection and love from the men who expressed interest, with her commitment to her marriage.

Working to understand what was a soulful desire and what was an egoic need was challenging, but when she took responsibility for her experience, she understood the truth. As a child, Leigha didn't receive the love she needed from her father. As a result, an 'insatiable little girl' developed as part of her constructed self. A little girl who wanted to dance and play and get piggyback rides. A little girl who craved quality time. A little girl who needed more love. When Leigha took responsibility for this part of herself, she realized that the only love that would satisfy the insatiable little girl was her own. She let her soul take the lead by taking responsibility. She had bold conversations with these men about how she was searching for her father's love in their attention and how she needed to step away to focus on loving herself. Then, she shared the truth with her husband about what she had experienced and how she was going to focus on giving herself the love she needed. "We have to take responsibility for ourselves and our lives," says Leigha. "We have to put our soul in the driver's seat."

* * *

Reflection softens the hard edge of responsibility. Being reflective means looking deep within yourself and your life to uncover how you can be the most authentic version of you. It means showing up for yourself by being curious about, and reflecting on, what's happening beneath the surface. The energy that guides your life exists in the depths – and it is there you must go.

Engage in reflection, examine the repetitive thoughts, core beliefs, defenses and stories that emerge when you are unconscious or suffering. I believe, with all my heart, that conscious reflection leads to liberation. Living with responsibility and reflection can be scary. Far more terrifying, though, is reaching the end of your days and realizing you let fear stop you from living a life you love.

What are the hidden motives behind the choices you make?

What are you pretending not to know?

When I think about living with courage, I feel ...

If I was engaging reflectively with my life, I would ...

If I took responsibility for my life, I would stop ...

COMMUNITY

Reminding one another of the dream that each of us aspires to may be enough for us to set each other free.

ANTOINE DE SAINT-EXUPERY

The individualistic and self-reliant nature of life design requires we bring some balance to the equation with a heavy emphasis on community. Community matters for two reasons. First, feeling a sense of connection and belonging is a fundamental human need. Second, we can accomplish much more together than we can on our own.

Your Great Life was first shared with the world as a luxury retreat in the heart of the Rocky Mountains. A collection of like-minded people gathered with the intention of designing, and living, more soulful lives. Together we united in our common values of courage and consciousness, we got creative and we designed our lives. The weekend was profound, life-shaking, and soul-making. But, something was missing. Community.

The following year we tripled our size with the intention of creating a tribe of Life Designers. It was important not only to live lives we loved, but also to feel a sense of connection and belonging as we leapt out into the unknown.

The life design tribe is one of the greatest gifts that this work has given me. With community support, it's easier to leap over hurdles, tear down walls, and dissolve blocks. In our community, we have supported each other though life's most challenging obstacles: bankruptcy, death, divorce, depression, addiction, and fear. We have also celebrated life's most precious moments: births, new beginnings, marriage, travel adventures, exciting endeavors, new businesses, inspiring romances, and deepening friendships.

Our society is moving faster than ever before, and while we're more connected, we are also more detached. Technology, social media, busy schedules, shifting careers and frequent relocations can make it increasingly difficult to create a sense of community. When we lack community, we tend to feel isolated, and isolation leads to loneliness and depression. Overall, when people experience fragmentation and detachment, we see more violence, substance abuse, and mental illness. A strong community gives you a sense of connection, belonging, love, and support – and it adds to the love in the world.

* * *

Mabel, a real estate investor, deeply values connection. Over many years, she created a thriving community, close relationships, and feeling of belonging. When the opportunity emerged to move to a new city with a flourishing real estate investment market, Mabel took the leap. She followed the opportunity, but as a natural introvert, it was difficult for her to recreate a sense of connection and belonging.

For years, she lived without a feeling of community. She had relationships, but most of the relationships were centered on values that didn't matter to her. Mabel felt disconnected, guarded, and alone. With a sincere need to reconnect to herself and to a community, she escaped to the Rocky Mountains for a life design retreat and found her tribe. "People were so willing to connect in a deep and meaningful way by dropping pretence and having real conversations," says Mabel. "There was so much warmth, like hugs, eye contact, and creating space for me to feel what I was feeling. Everything went wide open inside. It was like nothing I've ever experienced before. Community is so important, and I no longer feel alone, disconnected and guarded. Having a community that knows what matters to me and offers me love and support is like being wrapped in a soft, warm blanket. Now my clan has broadened, both near and far."

Creating community wasn't always easy for Mabel. Here are some suggestions she offered to others struggling to find their tribes: "Go to the places where the people you want to be connected to gather. When you find something that really resonates with your soul, go out and do it, whether it's eco-issues, dancing, yoga, or book clubs. When you surround yourself with like-minded people, you will have an opportunity to find your tribe."

* * *

Don't wait for your community to find you. Reflect, explore, have courageous conversations, take action, and embrace thoughtful vulnerability. Create the conditions to build the community you need. When you set aside your masks and courageously let your true self emerge uncensored, unrehearsed, and unbridled, you become a beacon for like-minded people who are also seeking community. Only when you have the courage to be vulnerable will you draw in the people you need.

Although no life design journey will be exactly like yours, the power of tribe can give you strength when you're not sure you can take another step. Your community will help you to stay awake to the truth of your life. Unconscious living is a powerful force and it will lull you back to sleep if you let it. Your community will help to nudge you awake if you begin to drift off.

Your community will also support you in taking courageous action. When you see someone else leap into the unknown, it can inspire you to do the same. Your great life is not something that is completely created on your own. After all, we are human, and we are all in this together.

LIMBIC RESONANCE

The people in your community directly affect how much or how little you love your life. In chapter 10, we're going to design a blueprint you can build your life from, including an important process called limbic resonance. With limbic resonance, exposure to another person's blueprint creates a corresponding blueprint within you. Ongoing exposure to another person's blueprint will strengthen your matching blueprint. This is why we tend to be as happy, healthy, and successful as the people with whom we spend the most time. The people you are in relationship with and surround yourself with will change your heart and mind. Simply put, who we are and who we become is deeply connected to the community we spend time in and the people we love.

Limbic resonance allows us to bridge the gap between our minds, and it's what makes emotions feel contagious. We're all connected by our limbic systems, so we're automatically able to pull others into our emotional worlds.

Limbic resonance can be a powerful force or a challenging influence. Have you ever been around someone positive, loving, and uplifting? You leave the interaction feeling great! This is limbic resonance in motion. Yet, it can also be responsible for keeping us stuck in the muck. Let's pretend that you've been able to escape the clutches of depression through therapy and personal reflection. Then you go home to a family member, who also struggles with depression and, frustratingly, you relapse into the darkness. Limbic resonance can unintentionally provoke the historical blueprints that we are most eager to escape.

BELONGING

We all want to feel a sense of connection and belonging. We all want to be seen and appreciated for who we really are. In every moment of every day, we are co-creating our lives with the people around us. When building community, it's important to consider the kind of community you want to join. This doesn't mean we cut people out of our lives because their blueprints don't match or support our own, though you might discover that's necessary. Instead, it means we consciously engage with the truth of who we are and the life we want to live. We find ways to create meaningful connections based on what matters most.

As you awaken to the truth of your soul and you set out to live a life you love, it is necessary to find where you belong and to nurture a sense of unity. There is a little voice inside each of us that wants to be heard. It cries when it feels excluded and it aches to belong. Desiring deep connections is a natural human longing. Follow the pull. Be where you belong.

When I think about living with community, I feel ...

The community I want to belong to is ...

In order to connect with my tribe, I will ...

CHAPTER FIVE

THE SACRED ADVENTURE

The biggest adventure you can ever take is to live the life of your dreams.

OPRAH WINFREY

SACRED: AN ACT OF DEVOTION; REGARDED WITH REVERENCE; DIVINE, transcendent, holy; worthy of awe, reverence or respect; at the core of existence and has a transformative effect on life.

Adventure : an exciting experience; a bold, potentially risky undertaking; a journey with an uncertain outcome; a major pursuit in and of itself; anything that's exciting, challenging, rewarding; a way to gain wisdom, life experience, and knowledge; starts with the call to have an unusual experience; exploration of unknown territory; to dare; to risk; to proceed despite the challenges.

Living is a sacred act.

Conscious living is an adventure.

Life design is about choosing the sacred adventure over the well-worn path.

Choosing the sacred adventure leads to greater freedom and authenticity. But, as with any adventure, we can't know what we will stumble across. There may be twists and turns, unexpected detours, and at times the obstacles may feel insurmountable. The risk and challenge is worth it.

If we don't enter into the adventure of soulful reflection and conscious life design, we tend to seek comfort over greatness, safety over risk, reassurance over authenticity, the predictable over the unknown, and the well-worn path over forging our own.

* * *

Jackie Dumaine was sitting in her car on a cold and grey day. She was paralyzed with fear and anxiety, questioning whether or not she wanted to continue living. Burned out from a high stress career in advertising sales that was slowly breaking her spirit, she knew that the life she had known needed to end. With the help of quality questions and divine guidance, Jackie became aware of her soul's truth, and she gathered the courage to embark on a new path. A few months later, Jackie left her six-figure career and traveled to an ashram in India where she studied yoga and meditation. When she returned to Canada, she became inspired to translate the ancient teachings of yogic texts for our modern world, so she created The Yoga Code. "It was so clear that this was what I needed to do," says Jackie. "Just the thought of it made me feel so alive."

* * *

When you choose to design a life you love, you are committing to be in a conscious relationship with your soul. You are adventuring into the rich jungle of your most authentic, meaningful, and fulfilled life.

Like most adventures, your great life isn't a destination. You never arrive. It's a way of being in our world and a way of creating your world. It is always in motion. It comes alive when you choose to stay awake to the truth of your soul. It thrives when you choose love, courage, and community over fear. Your great life lives in the moments you choose your soul over your ego – when you listen to the whispers of your true self over the hollering of your constructed self.

SELF-DETERMINATION

Life design is an adventure you choose for yourself. It's about defining yourself and your life on your own terms. Designing your life is a powerful act of self-love and self-determination. No matter what masks you have been wearing, how you've been disguising your truth, or how you've contorted yourself into becoming someone you are not, when you step into consciously designing a life you love, you are embracing your greatest power and your ultimate potential.

Don't design your life for others – not even the people you love the most, and not even if it means your heart will break a little. Design your life based on what you most desire. As I watch courageous life designers stepping into their great lives, they ultimately end up serving others in some way. But, first, they start by serving themselves.

The truth of every human's life lies deeply within the soul. When you redesign your life based on your truth, motivation, beliefs, actions, and feelings, you move in the direction of the life you love.

My sacred adventure includes ...

When choosing this sacred adventure, I am most afraid of ...

When choosing this sacred adventure, I am most excited for ...

CONFORMITY

You don't have to live your life the way other people expect you to.

CHRIS GUILLEBEAU

To conform is to align your attitudes, beliefs, and behaviors with those around you. Conformity is a powerful force that can sweep us away from the life we love through social pressure, unconscious influences, and common expectations.

Even though our culture and society are more liberated than ever before, we still experience tremendous pressure to conform. Stifling traditions, glass ceilings, suffocating expectations, limiting labels, restrictive stereotypes, and impossible standards can be difficult to avoid. The problem is not in their existence, but in our lack of conscious engagement with these influences. Our life force becomes dull and diminished when we fail to go within, reflect on the truth of who we are, and connect with our own internal compass. If we unconsciously accept, *this is just how things are,* we rob ourselves of the opportunity to live a truer life. When we consciously engage with the ways in which we're expected to conform and how these expectations affect us and shape our choices, we are better equipped to make choices that align with the truth of our soul rather than others' expectations.

We are all unique individuals and typically, life designers have a desire to live a distinctive life. Every choice we make is a unique expression of the life we want to live. You are hard-wired for unique self-expression. From the swirl in your fingertips to the twists in your DNA, the chance of finding your carbon copy is one in 400 trillion. You are uniquely you in every possible way. Doesn't it make sense that your life will also be profoundly unique?

On the other hand, we are also hard-wired for conformity. We are herd animals, so we feel safest in our pack. As a result, we are equipped to pick up on social cues, coordinate ourselves according to expectations, and align our lives with those around us. Social disapproval sets off the danger circuits and when we conform, we are soothed. Unfortunately, just because our biology favors conformity, doesn't mean our souls are equally pacified.

When we live our lives from the truth of our soul, we experience more peace, fulfillment, and energy. When we don't, we experience more turmoil, emptiness, and lethargy. Struggling and suffering often escalate when the soul refuses to conform to thoughts, choices, and priorities that betray its strongest desires.

You are not the roles, standards, and behaviors you are expected to express. There is a real you in the depths – a part of yourself that knows what deeply matters. You may find conformity is what your true self wants, and I'm not asking you to live an unconventional life just for the sake of it. Rather, life design is a process of being aware of the overt and subtle influences of conformity and consciously choosing to adhere to them or not.

When we consume the fast food of social expectations and unconscious conformity, we become malnourished and our lives grow toxic. Our true self begins to starve, we lose our spark, our actions weaken, and our expression diminishes.

Our society trains us to keep up, to climb the corporate ladder even in we're not into heights, to have 2.5 children even if our soul doesn't long to be a parent, to perform better, achieve more, and look better at all costs. Climbing the corporate ladder, having children, getting higher grades, driving a faster car, or buying a bigger house might bring you soulful satisfaction, but only if you are consciously choosing this kind of life, and only if it's in harmony with your true self. Unexamined expectations and unconscious conformity are dangerous.

Conforming to the mainstream may feel purposeful and soulful. Designing a life you love may mean adhering to common courtesies, subscribing to meaningful traditions, and following the rules.

Alternatively, your soul may be calling you to an unconventional life. You may live outside the box, survive off the grid, and politely decline the status quo. If this sounds like you, pick up Chris Guillebeau's book, *The Art of Non-Conformity*, or check out his blog.

When you have an intimate relationship with your true self, it is easier to soulfully navigate outside forces and live a life you love.

In what area of your life are you most likely to live unconsciously?

What expectations, actions, or roles betray the truth of your soul?

Which roles in your life do you play for the sake of someone else?

What reflexive patterns do you conform to?

In designing my life the way I want it to be, I will conform by ...

In designing my life the way I want it to be, I will not conform by ...

YOUR LIFE IS THE HOME OF YOUR SOUL

Every moment I shape my destiny with a chisel, I am a carpenter of my own soul.

RUMI

Life design is a process of genuinely expressing who you are and the life you long to live. Designing a great life is a lot like designing a custom home. It starts with a thoughtful blueprint based on good science. When you decide to build a custom home, you are a co-creator. You're not moving into a house someone else designed for you. You are moving into a home that is exactly the way you want it to be.

When you build a custom home, you select your team based on the qualities you want in your home. Whether you want a log home in the mountains or a cottage by the sea, you will select an architect who knows the terrain and a builder with the skills required to create a home you will adore. You will gather art and accents to make it a space you never want to leave. Similarly, when you design your life, you will need to make meaningful connections with people who support you in building a life that you deeply love.

When you are building a custom home, you shape the blueprints, the building process, the decorating, and the experience of living in the home. You influence the shape, size and location. You select the materials, reflect on the construction process, and make changes along the way. You spend your precious time, money, and energy on your home and once it is built, you decorate it in a way that feels comfortable, peaceful, and welcoming to you. You design a sanctuary.

Custom home-builders will often tell you that great homes are built around your lifestyle, and so is a life you love. When you craft the blueprint of your great life, it's important to consciously choose a lifestyle that will nourish your heart, mind, and soul.

Your life is the home of your soul. Is your soul living in a cookie-cutter house? If so, you might feel like something is missing; it's not completely home. You might wish the rooms you rest in had more light, and when you open the door, you long for a wider hallway. Perhaps there's not enough time, money, or energy to knock out a wall and add an atrium, but it would make things a whole lot better.

A home is not a custom home unless it has your unique touch. A life is not a great life unless it reflects the unique qualities of your soul. Avoiding a cookie-cutter life takes awareness and determination. You are still subject to the conditions of modern reality: beauty magazines that make you feel ugly, corporate policies that button you up, pressures to be 'realistic,' and past baggage you've been dragging. It's easy for your true self to suffocate beneath a pile of expectations, confusion, and conformity.

Sometimes, when we begin the life design process, a simple renovation will do. Renovations are in order if the home of your soul no longer aligns with your values or lifestyle.

On the other hand, sometimes a renovation won't do. If there's a problem with the foundation, everything may need to go. This was my story. When I woke up to the awareness that we, the relatively privileged, have the power to design our lives the way we want them to be, I began to see how my life was inauthentic. I was living in a cookie-cutter house built upon the perilous foundation of fear. I thought it all had to be destroyed, so that's what I did. I ended my relationship, lost my friends, adopted my pets, gave up my house, quit my jobs, divided my assets, and shattered my sense of self. I was alone and homeless and free. The false structures of my life crumbled around me and I found myself in a pile of rubble and ruin. Amongst all of this loss, I felt liberated.

I lost my life, as I knew it to be, but I found my soul. Life wasn't sunshine and rainbows from this point forward. I still continued to repress my true self and build false structures. The difference was, I was conscious. I would see patterns and recognize the symptoms of a suffering soul. I had embraced an insatiable longing – to be authentic at all costs and to design a life my soul wanted to call home.

If we live in an inauthentic life for an extended period of time, our cookie-cutter house may transform into a prison. If we've sacrificed our true self for long enough, we can feel like we are prisoners in someone else's life, because we are. The beliefs, opinions, judgments, and expectations of others become bars that confine us. Over time, our ego accepts the bars as our own and we become both the prison and the prisoner. When we have allowed ourselves to live in prisons built by others or by the lies of the constructed self, we often need a dramatic wake-up call to realize we've been holding the key the whole time.

Is your life a custom home, a cookie-cutter home, or a prison?

The places in my life that feel constricting are ...

The lifestyle I want to build my life around is ...

I'd like to escape from ...

The life I feel most at home in includes ...

A custom home is a product
of invention, creativity,
imagination, and intention.
We are each the designers
in our own lives. Will you
design something conventional
and ordinary or something
remarkable and extraordinary?
It’s up to you.

CHAPTER SIX

SOMETHING IS WRONG WITH MY LIFE

I believe that the glimmering slice of truth - call it your soul, unabashed love, the unfettered wishes and dreams that have long remained nestled in your heart but remain hidden for fear, guilt or shame - is where you have to live from.

DAVE URSILLO

THE LIFE YOU LOVE WILL CALL TO YOU IN MANY WAYS. SOMETIMES WE FEEL a yearning, a longing, a desire, or a happy anticipation. Other times, something goes wrong, like illness, boredom, depression, drama, addiction, anxiety, chaos, adrenal fatigue, nightmares, apathy, chronic distraction, mindless consumption, feeling unfulfilled, agitation, hopelessness, helplessness, an armored heart, dull eyes, or lack of presence. The soul expresses its dissatisfaction in many ways.

As a psychologist, I often counsel people who struggle with mental and emotional challenges. Psychopathology is the collective definition of various psychological problems and dysfunctions. Although I work with people who suffer from psychopathology, I resist the clinical definition. Instead, I've chosen to align with the meaning of psychopathology, which is, expressing the suffering of a soul. When we do what the soul does not want us to do, we suffer. The symptoms are often a painful sign that we need to discover where we took a wrong turn.

Søren Kierkegaard, a Danish philosopher with a fondness for psychology, believed anxiety, boredom, and despair were all remedied by choosing to be who we really are. Indeed, the most important quest we can take is to live our lives with truth, authenticity, and soulful alignment.

* * *

Briana's story of anxiety, depression and addiction began in her teens. Until the age of 14 she was considered a normal, healthy, athletic teenager. In the matter of one month, everything changed and she was unable to function.

Briana was paranoid and felt like everyone she encountered was judging her – and that fear of judgment was so intense, she hated waking up in the morning.

Her mother took her to the family doctor, who prescribed antidepressants, and from that point forward Briana moved through life feeling numb and sad. She began comforting herself with food and she became dependent on marijuana and alcohol to sleep.

In an attempt to escape, Briana would lock herself in her room and pass the time by making jewelry from anything she could find. When she was around others, she would immediately feel anxious and angry.

Despite the tremendous challenges in her life, Briana started college, where her drinking, overeating and drug use skyrocketed. Every night, she drank and used drugs to escape the anxiety under her skin and the heaviness in her heart. From the outside looking in, it seemed like she was having a great time and partying like every other college student. The addictions hid the depth of her suffering.

After college, Briana got a job in a field that didn't interest her. She spent the years that followed in a deep state of unhappiness, which grew to the point where she was drinking and taking sleeping pills every night. "I remember driving down the street after work, in an almost full-blown panic, looking for someone to sell me drugs," says Briana. "I didn't care what it was – I just needed to escape from this overwhelming, suffocating pain. If someone had offered me heroin, I would have taken it without a second thought. Thankfully, no one did."

Briana started to question the point of living; she didn't understand why she was born or see her purpose on this planet. The thought of living this way for another 50 years was unbearable, and her survival depended on finding a life she loved. Briana's life design began with searching for answers, discovering why she was suffering, and uncovering the pain she had repressed. Once she healed the past, she designed her great future.

As she began to design her life, Briana stumbled upon a comforting fact: facing the discomfort and dealing with the difficult days wasn't as unmanageable as she thought it would be. Facing the pain worked better than numbing the pain. On the sacred adventure of designing a life she loved, Briana began committing to daily acts of self-love, and she treated herself gently and with compassion. Reminding herself to focus on the good, express gratitude, and pay attention to the whispering of her soul were the keys to her salvation.

The more Briana tuned in and listened to the desire of her true self, the more she connected with the actions she needed to take in order to live a life she loved. One day, during a conversation with her sister, Briana realized that her soul craved creative expression. Her path became clear and she started making art.

Part of Briana's great life involved committing to a daily meditation practice. In the beginning, Briana was unable to quiet her thoughts enough to focus on her breath, so she grabbed a set of mala beads to distract her busy mind. Using malas to support her meditation practice allowed Briana to retrain her brain and moved her thinking from dark to light.

Soon, Briana combined her love of creative expression with the tool that helped to calm her mind. She designed and created meditation malas from her favorite gemstone beads. People began noticing, and complimenting, the malas she wore. Requests for her malas started to flow in.

The love Briana received from following her passion and creating her art was beautiful and overwhelming. Suddenly, she had a community of people who cared about her and supported her.

By finding her true self and committing to the sacred adventure of designing her life, Briana was able to overcome her need to self-soothe with food, alcohol, drugs, and prescription medication.

"Now I am living my great life," says Briana. "I meditate daily and take time to have my bare feet on the earth. My business, Precious Malas, is thriving and I'm so grateful to be building a life around my calling and passion. I am living in gratitude and I make an effort to love myself every day. It has had a ripple effect, because the more I am able to love and accept myself, the more I can love and accept others. I nourish my body instead of abusing it. I have learned to listen to the quiet voice guiding me to the needs of my heart and soul. When I listen to that voice I am at peace."

* * *

My clients usually come to me when something is wrong with their lives – they are struggling with fear, anxiety, or depression and sometimes they have been hit with a devastating crisis. Occasionally, they are medicated or addicted and don't want to be numb anymore. In many ways, these challenges often call for a life design.

LIFE DESIGN AND DEPRESSION

We commonly hear about two kinds of depression: biologically-based depression and reactive depression. Biological depression is passed down genetically and is best treated with a combination of medication and short-term therapy. Reactive depression is usually brought on by a significant life change – the death of a loved one, divorce, kids heading off to college, retirement, a serious car accident, economic instability, and so on. To treat reactive depression, we need to process the life change and redirect the energy in an empowering and meaningful way. This requires personal awareness, psychological honesty, emotional integrity, and sometimes, the guidance of a therapist.

The third type of depression I see in my practice is the most common, and it's rarely discussed. It's so subtle that most people who suffer from it don't even know they have it. This depression includes a general blah feeling, difficulty feeling happy, lackluster feelings about life, and waking up feeling like it's time to tackle another difficult day.

I believe this state originates from a battle between the life the true self wants us to live and the life the constructed self is leading. The true self feeds our energy, and if it's dissatisfied for long enough, it will cut off the flow of energy and depression soon sets in.

When I am discontented in my life, it's because ...

What's not working about my life is ...

I feel disconnection in my life when ...

I am self-critical when ...

I feel drained when ...

LIFE DESIGN AND ADDICTION

When we are not living the life we love, there's often a longing to escape. There are two kinds of escaping. The soulful escape is an experience where you grow wildly into your life and you are no longer contained by outside forces, false constructs, or meaningless expectations.

The constructed self, however, often tries to escape through some type of addiction. It may be an addiction to a chemical substance or it could be a non-clinical type of addiction. Any reflexive response to stress, anxiety, uncertainty, or emotional pain is an addiction, such as zoning out with The Bachelor, taking the edge off with a glass of wine, compulsive eating or exercising, reading Fifty Shades of Grey again, joining the cult of the eternally busy, creating drama, or taking another vacation you can't afford. These are all addictive coping strategies.

Early in my career, I found myself working for an organization that supported children with severe behaviors, who had been removed from every other system and landed in my office. As a play therapist, I saw tragedy and trauma play out in the sand tray multiple times a day. This position devastated my sensitive soul. After three years, my depression was at an all-time high. I had ignored the messages from my soul for years, until they became impossible to tune out. One morning, before the children arrived, I became still and surrendered. The whispers grew louder: *this is not your life. It's your mom's life. This isn't your calling. You are meant for something different. Only when you are true to yourself will this suffering go away.* My mom was also a play therapist and while she never told me what work to do, I was so disconnected from my true self that I fell into what was most familiar. Day after day of living someone else's life caught up with me. On my way home from work, I would stop by the convenience store and buy a pint of ice cream. I ate in a desperate attempt to numb the suffering, but there was no relief at the bottom of that bucket. Soon, tubs of ice cream turned into bottles of wine. The struggle didn't stop until I listened.

When we deplete our soul we feel hungry, forever grasping for more, and desperately miserable. We awful-ize life and we try to fill the gaping hole with anything we can find – Ben & Jerry's, *Desperate Housewives*, Facebook, merlot, cocaine, sex, shoes. We are tempted and seduced by anything that may fill us, yet we continue to starve. We try to escape the symptoms, but in truth, all that's required is genuine acceptance that we cannot escape the truth of our souls.

Addictive coping strategies allow us to avoid feeling what we are feeling and distract us from what's going on beneath the surface. They momentarily push back the darkness and let us stop feeling what's uncomfortable, if only for a few minutes. And yet, addictive coping strategies only prolong suffering.

Releasing the addiction requires us to feel what we are feeling – even if it's painful. Once we have felt what we needed to feel, we have more information to make a truthful choice and to move in the direction of living a life we love. By deepening our awareness of what we feel and what we need, we are free to choose conscious living over unconscious addiction. Freedom follows.

I know you didn't come to this life to numb out with a bottle of wine and four hours of television every night. You didn't come here to sleep through your life and wake up with regret right before you die. You did not come here to live an untrue life. You came to live a life you love and to do what deeply matters.

What addictive tendency do you turn to?

Before you engage in your addiction, ask yourself ...

What am I avoiding?

What's not working about my life is ...

What do I not want to feel?

What might happen if I allow myself to feel it?

What do I really need?

How can I choose something more soulful?

LIFE DESIGN AND CRISIS

Sometimes a crisis is a summons to reconfigure our entire life. Even though we are resilient creatures, we are easily hurt and there are times when living hurts. A lot.

There is purpose in pain. Often, life falls apart exactly when it needs to be rebuilt. Pain sets in when our stories become burdensome and our defense mechanisms become draining. When we are no longer able to maintain the stories and defenses that protect us, we can feel overwhelmed by life's mental, physical, emotional, and spiritual struggles.

When life collapses, it's the perfect opportunity to design and build something newer, truer, and fuller.

* * *

It was Valentine's Day and Farhana, a mom of three young children, had just learned that her husband of 10 years had purchased a gift for another woman. She was numb. She drifted through her day with heaviness in her heart and she hung onto denial like it was her last friend in the world.

Farhana couldn't bear the thought of her world disintegrating. In shock, she asked her husband about it when he came home. Even though she had tangible evidence in her hands, she desperately wanted to believe his convincing denials and mask of sincerity.

Farhana realized that she never really wanted to see the truth. Until she did. Eventually, her husband exhausted his capacity for denial and admitted to purchasing a gift for the woman who had haunted their marriage for years.

As Farhana's life crumbled, she began to see it as a catalyst for transformation. She courageously ventured within herself and emerged glowing in the truth of her soul. After Farhana redesigned her life, she wrote a book about her experience, called *Thank You For Leaving Me* – a heartfelt, refreshingly real account of her journey through divorce and life design.

* * *

We all experience feelings of loss, confusion, discomfort, and heartbreak. At times, it can feel inconvenient to feel what we are feeling. Farhana's crisis quickly threw her into life as a single mom of three small children who needed care and financial support. Crisis can be processed while you are making dinner or driving to work; the key is to maintain a level of presence by asking yourself, *how am I really feeling? What deeply matters to me now?* If you only have 10 minutes while you're washing the dishes, take those 10 minutes. Allow your automatic mind to take over the dishwashing while you settle into your breathing and connect with your soul.

When you attune to what is real, you are more able to float with the flow of your true self, rather than struggling against it. When we stop resisting or repressing our experiences, we can process our feelings more quickly and completely. When we struggle against crisis, we make ourselves vulnerable to fearful living.

Fear controls much of our lives and defense mechanisms are by-products of fear. We avoid, deny, repress, numb, blame, and project. We flee from personal responsibility and refuse to accept reality. We defer to a perceived authority figure and give our power to others. We sacrifice our true self and ignore our soul's calling. We get worked up over trivial issues. We seek validation and need approval. We get hard, we go cold, we shut out love. We distract ourselves with television, work, or busyness. We numb out with our drug of choice. We compartmentalize the places in our lives that are out of alignment and we rationalize our fearful choices.

These defense mechanisms push us deeper into unconscious living and suffering.

As long as we choose this path, we will continue to feel lost. No defense can protect us from the rawness of life. No wall can keep out the pain. In fact, the defenses and walls cause the rawness and pain to linger. The truth is, when we release the defenses and break down the walls, the rawness and pain can pass through more freely and make way for relief and freedom. Standing up to fear and shedding defense mechanisms is the most critical choice you can make on the path to healing, wholeness, and a more fulfilling life.

BREAK DOWN OR BREAK OPEN

During times of crisis, we have the choice to break down or break open. When we allow ourselves to stay open and experience the pain in a healthy way, we open ourselves to the process of designing a life we love.

The desire to avoid pain is natural, but if we allow pain to shut us down, we close off to the possibility of entering into a richer, more authentic way of living. Rumi, and other great mystics, wrote poetic prose about how a broken heart is an open heart. Fully feeling heartbreak and not closing down to pain allows for joy and wisdom to enter in through the cracks.

When you are in a crisis and wanting to emerge into life design, the wisest and kindest thing you can do for yourself is to slow down. If you rush through it, the insights and awareness will slip by unnoticed.

As uncomfortable as it is, feel what you are feeling. When you notice the urge to distract or deflect the discomfort, gently pull yourself back into the feeling and breathe through it. Find a way to support yourself through this time without running away from reality. Dance, meditation, bodywork, writing, yoga, creative expression, time in nature, psychotherapy, and breath work are all healthy ways to process pain and integrate the experience by accepting it and finding meaning in it.

Who was I before this crisis?

Who am I after this crisis?

How can I let this crisis open me?

What do you really love about your life and why?

I know that designing a life you love is not always easy. Our culture often prevents us from growing into our true selves. We are pressured to know what we will be when we grow up long before we've actually grown up. We're expected to conform to the status quo of education, employment, and marriage before we've explored our inner world and the outer world.

How can we know what we do not know? In the absence of our own knowing, we conform to the path others have laid for us. We choose a career, political party, religion, and life partner based on a socially acceptable version of a good life and, in the process, we miss out on our great life.

The unconscious pull of our family and our culture is strong. Unless our internal knowing and self-awareness is highly developed, we can be swept into an inauthentic way of living. These, sometimes painful, reminders from the soul serve to keep us as close to our true path as possible.

CHAPTER SEVEN

LETTING GO OF THE OLD

But little by little, as you left their voices behind, the stars began to burn through the sheets of clouds, and there was a new voice which you slowly recognized as your own, that kept you company as you strode deeper and deeper into the world determined to do the only thing you could do — determined to save the only life you could save.

MARY OLIVER

WHEN YOU ARE ON THE ROAD TO SAVING THE ONLY LIFE YOU CAN save, there will be many moments of letting go. Letting go doesn't always mean an ending to what was. I've seen people design their lives and end up divorced, and I've seen people design their lives and transform their marriages in the process. I've seen people leave their soul-sucking job and I've seen people negotiate their work into something more meaningful and fulfilling. Even if your life design does not call you to end something, you will still need to let go of some things.

You may need to let go of old ways of thinking, distractions, clutter, needing to be right, unhealthy patterns, avoiding the unknown, restricting roles, grudges, a limiting label, resentment, fearful beliefs, stifling possessions, or a part of your identity.

My son was three when he started his pre-school Montessori program. The first days of school were difficult for him. He cried so hard, he could barely breathe, and his little chest heaved intensely while teardrops streamed down his face. He didn't want to let go. He liked the life he had – unlimited hours at the park, cuddles available anytime he wanted, a parent with him everywhere he went. The life he knew was safe, familiar, and predictable.

It's difficult to see our children in painful transitions, but deep down, we know we must let them go through these shifts so they can live their lives. As parents, we need to let go of our children and encourage them to do hard things. We need to do the same for ourselves.

Letting go is a skill you will continue to develop as you design your life. When we don't let go of our children, we cause them harm. When we don't let go of that which no longer serves us, we harm ourselves.

Letting go starts with recognizing the belief behind what you are clutching so tightly. Usually, that belief is connected to happiness. My little boy believed he needed to be with his parents all the time in order to be happy. What belief do you have about your happiness that is preventing you from letting go?

Once you recognize the belief, it's time to fully embrace the truth – that you don't need any one person or any one thing in order to be happy. It doesn't matter how attached you are, your happiness is not inextricably linked to something outside yourself. Paradoxically, once you let go, it's much easier to enjoy the people and things you want to hold onto. After a few days of struggling to let go, my little one embraced the truth – that time with his parents can make him happy and time with his friends can make him happy, too.

Designing a life you love does not mean tightly gripping something or someone, no matter how much you may desire it and no matter how much you may love them. When you are willing to let go, you become free to design your life the way you want it to be.

TRUST

When I first began university, it quickly became clear that the timing was not right. I isolated myself, sank into a deep depression, and almost failed my classes. After one semester I knew I needed something different so, of course, I signed up to save the world! A few months later I found myself in Guyana – a land of breathtaking natural beauty, rich heritage, and kind people. I joined a group of do-gooding young adults and we adventured into the unknown. We lived in a small village nestled on the edge of a lush jungle and tried our best to be helpful. One humid afternoon, I was invited on a jungle walk. As we trekked into the wilderness, we stumbled upon a troop of monkeys swinging through the trees. I was enamored with one particularly cheeky monkey, so I pulled up a log and watched her for a while. As she swung, there was a brief moment where she had to let go before finding security on the next vine. She had to trust that what she was planning to grasp would be secure, and if it wasn't, she had to trust she would find another option before hitting the ground.

Moving from your present life into the life you love is very similar. There is a period of time where it may feel like you have nothing solid to grasp. It may feel insecure or uncertain. Of course, you will make the best decisions you can with what you know and the resources that are available to you, but ultimately, the most important thing you can do is to be in a state of trust. As Goethe says, *as soon as you trust yourself, you will know how to live.*

In order to muster the strength and courage to let go, it can be helpful to remember, you've done this before. The person you are now is very different from the person you have been. You have lost relationships, broken habits, released emotions, reinvented part of your identity, and surrendered old roles. You've navigated loss before and you can do it again.

How have you changed in the last five years?

What do you believe now that you didn't believe then?

What do you accept now that you didn't accept then?

What have you outgrown?

What have you left behind?

You may need to give up a long-held belief, quit a job, leave the country, end a relationship, release a destructive pattern, surrender your old sense of self, or abandon a role that no longer fits.

* * *

Shelley battled with her weight for years. She hired many trainers and did exactly as she was told. She tried countless diets and followed them precisely. Ingesting expensive supplements only worked temporarily, despite her dedication and commitment to each new regimen. Shelley pushed herself to achieve something external – an appearance that was accepted by society – and she eventually experienced adrenal fatigue.

After another round with a trainer she really loved, it became clear to her there was more to life than following a diet and exercise program. Shelley tuned into her soul and realized there was a profound disconnection between her head, heart, and body. She knew that until she worked on her internal world, her external world wouldn't change. What her head wanted was completely different from what her soul was craving.

The fitness world told her she was making excuses, but Shelley knew her truth. When she followed the path others had laid out for her, she struggled. When she followed her own path and listened to her soul, she loved her body and healed her heart. She reclaimed her life and her health by finding her truth and learning to trust it. "What if your soul was the only mentor you ever needed to hire?" says Shelley. "Maybe it is. Your soul always knows what is true and what is not. You know in your soul whether you are on the right path or not. Do you feel like throwing up or dancing? Do what makes you feel like dancing."

* * *

Once you choose the truth of your soul, it can be very difficult to remain in anything that feels inauthentic. Your work may start to feel false, your true self may ask you to find another place to call home, and your relationships may start to feel too small. These sensations emerge when the full expression of your essence is constricted in some way.

A calm sadness may settle in when you realize there are elements of your present that will not be part of your future. The space between the death of the old world and the birth of the new can be lonely and uncertain. You will have to let go and you may have to grieve.

Designing your life is about uncovering what is true for you and finding the courage to express it in the world. As you begin to live in the world in a new way, the old way will have to die. It's important to let the old world go with love. As we design our lives the way we want them to be, we must remain respectful of the rights and perspectives of others. They may be confused or scared once your life starts to change. Often they come around, but occasionally they do not. Either way, your new world will embrace you.

* * *

Olivia, a speech-language pathologist and mother of two small children, was in a verbally and emotionally abusive relationship. Every day her husband bombarded her with criticism about how she didn't measure up to his expectations. Over the years, she slowly began to lose her sense of self. Olivia didn't know who she was; she only knew she was never good enough.

For Olivia, knowing that her children were living in an emotionally toxic environment and she was unable to be the mother and woman they needed was the worst part of the situation. She desperately tried to fix the relationship by attending workshops and working with half a dozen therapists, hoping someone might be able to solve her problems and repair her marriage. Olivia's aha moment came after telling a therapist everything she was not, when the therapist asked, "Who are you?"

In this defining moment, Olivia realized she had no idea. She had spent so long failing to meet her husband's expectations that she had completely lost her sense of self. Before her next therapy appointment, Olivia sat down and made a list of everything she knew about herself. From that point forward, Olivia no longer allowed herself to be defined by her supposed shortcomings.

She made a commitment to be herself and to trust that she was enough. "Knowing my soul, and owning who I am," says Olivia, "was the catalyst that catapulted me into a life I love."

Olivia decided to be herself at all costs. That choice ended her marriage, but she saved herself, and her children now see the playful, courageous, engaged mother she really is.

The people who know and love Olivia delight in seeing that her sparkle has returned. "I am reconnected to who I am," says Olivia. "There's something so magical in being me, something I had lost and now I've found." The more Olivia connected to her true self, the more she was able to express it in the world. She started a gratitude journal and began practicing random acts of kindness. "Releasing who I was supposed to be freed me to be who I am," she says. "When I became aware of my true self, I was able to offer it to the world. I was surprised to discover what I have to give and how valuable it is to others."

In her marriage, Olivia heard repeatedly that she wasn't kind, loving or generous enough. By freeing herself from the confines of judgment and listening to her own voice, Olivia realized she was, in fact, deeply kind and caring. "Rejection no longer defines me and it doesn't control me," says Olivia. "As a result, I'm more able to be vulnerable and reach out to others. For example, I buy myself a fancy latte on my birthday every year as a treat to myself. When my birthday came around after I designed my life, I also bought a latte for the person in line behind me. I was so surprised by how this small act of kindness ignited my soul. It's so much easier now to show kindness. Before I designed my life, I wouldn't have been vulnerable like this. I was so uncomfortable with myself I didn't want to put myself out there for fear of being seen and judged as not good enough."

When Olivia designed her life, she became aware of the truth: by knowing who she is and living from a place of authenticity and alignment, she is able to live a more meaningful life. "It's not just another day or another coffee," says Olivia. "It's a sacred moment. A moment to celebrate. I want to make the small, simple moments matter. I want to live with intention."

* * *

When you are in the middle of uncertainty, you may feel an urge to do something, but it is important to be rather than to do. Spend time in nature, live in your breath, be creative without creating anything. By surrendering to the unknown and being in uncertainty, you honor the end of what was, and you create space to fully integrate the lessons of the past.

Sometimes letting go is easy, other times it is not. Learning to let go is one of the most important skills you can develop while designing a life you love. You may choose to let go of possessions, roles, or relationships. Or you may choose to let go of past emotions. Shame, blame, resentment and rage are toxic emotions, and if they linger for long enough, they will sabotage your desire to live a life you love. There are many ways to process emotions, so I encourage you to experiment with and explore what works for you.

When you have let go of what's familiar, you may find yourself in an unfamiliar place. Try asking yourself, what am I feeling? Let it rise up. Focus on your breathing and consciously deepen it. As you deepen your breath, reflect on all the information you can gather about the emotion: thoughts, sensations, beliefs, insights. Our bodies are able to process emotions much more effectively than our minds. Your hands, feet and voice can express and release emotional energy. Experiment with different releasing processes, like writing your emotions on a sheet of paper and then burning it, dancing, painting, going for a run, verbally expressing your feelings, throwing rocks in the ocean, or shaking your body. If you aren't sure what works for you, try them all.

THE EDGE

As you continue to move away from the old world and into your new world, you will encounter many edges. Reaching your edge is the experience of coming to an unknown, uncomfortable, or unfamiliar place – also known as the edge of your comfort zone. When you arrive at an edge, you may leap, pause, or take a step back. Despite the popular adage, "leap and a net will appear" or "you'll learn to fly," your truth may be different.

I have watched many life designers pause in the chaos of their present life. They allowed the present to be as it was and reflected on it from all perspectives. By taking time to reflect, you can more clearly see what you need to see in order to let go of what you need to surrender.

There are times to leap. There are times to pause. There are times to step back. Let your true self make the call, because somehow, it knows what's required for you to become who you really are and to live a life you love.

When I feel uncertain, I will remind myself ...

When I am in the unknown, I will focus on being ...

AND THEN, YOU HAVE TO DO IT

It takes a lot of courage to release the familiar and seemingly secure to embrace the new. But there is no real security in what is no longer meaningful. There is more security in the adventurous and in the exciting, for in movement there is life and in change there is power.

ALAN COHEN

Once you've taken the time to reflect on what needs to change, spent time being in the unknown, released your attachment to the outcome, and stopped trying to control what you can't control, it's time to do something. That's right. Do it.

I'm not asking you to let go of that big thing you know you want to release, though eventually it might be a good idea. Start with something small that doesn't freak you out. What's the easiest thing you can let go of? Start with that.

When I was a child, we lived on a small hobby farm, and every few years we would burn the grass around our property. Within a few short weeks, tender green shoots would emerge from the ashes. The same is true for our lives. The death of the old makes space for the new. Don't turn away from the sparks that will ignite the flame, even if you fear the blaze. In the ashes of destruction you will find the sprouts of new life. There are times to light the fire and times to let life grow. Only your soul knows the right season. But, for now, let's step into the fire.

Try letting go of something every week that doesn't align with the design of your life: an unwanted possession, a limiting belief, an annoying thought, a pesky habit, a stack of clutter, a heavy obligation, an annoying social media account, or a restricting perception.

You might go through your wardrobe and weed out clothes that no longer fit. Or you might finally dump the clutter from the drawer that mysteriously collects junk. Purge if you need to purge. Making space in your physical world will make space in your mental world. Donate the books you no longer want. Revive or up-cycle material bits to match the design of your life. Give away the accessories that no longer make you feel how you want to feel.

What can you delegate? You are capable and talented and there are many things you can do. Just because you can do them, doesn't mean you should do them. Maybe it's time to let go of the old habit of doing it all yourself? How can you find the support you need and free yourself to live a life you love?

The parts of my life that feel least aligned are ...

If you don't let go of these parts, what will it do to you and your life?

I need to release and remove a few things from my world, including...

By letting go of these things I am making space to bring in ...

Before we design your life, we need to get clear about which internal obstacles are preventing you from living a life you love. It's time for you to meet all of you – not just the amazing, wonderful, and powerful parts, but also the less 'desirable' parts. Approach this task with the intention to be totally and completely honest with yourself.

We're going to explore what has been guiding your life up to this point. This process can be exciting, uplifting, and enlightening. It can also be unnerving, disorienting, and surprising. The question you can ask yourself now is, how far am I willing to go to know myself? I hope you are willing to delve deep into this process so you can uncover your true self and embrace the freedom to live a life you love.

You may find that the first word that comes to mind is a label, like mother, father, doctor, entrepreneur, Canadian, Christian, runner, yogi.

You are not only that, who are you?

Dig deeper into your answers by reflecting on your whole being. Are you only a lawyer, brother, friend, wife, cleaner, truck driver, or are you more than a label?

Who are you?

You are not only that, who are you?

Do you really need to be married, demanding, thoughtful, athletic, kind, atheist, unemployed or rich in order to be you?

Who are you?

You are not only that, who are you?

Set a timer for 10 minutes and write until it stops. Repeat the process and go deeper each time. Whatever you do, don't stop writing. If answers aren't coming, write the question "who am I?" and do your best to respond.

Allow your beliefs to bubble up to the surface. What do you believe about yourself?

Beliefs often sound like sweeping, generalized statements. Here are some beliefs I gathered from the life design tribe:

I am powerful. I am afraid of change. I am creative. I hate myself. I am not good at follow-through. I deserve to be loved. I am not loveable. I am fat. I am bubbly. I thrive during times of change. I am what other people think I am. I am an unhappy person. I know who I am. I need to make others happy. I am committed to my happiness and health.

Set a timer for 10 minutes and write until it stops. If the answers aren't coming, write the question "what do I believe about myself?" and do your best to respond.

What do you believe about living a life you love?

The beliefs and labels you subscribe to create the reality of your life. The stronger your belief, the more diligently your mind searches for evidence to prove it is accurate.

Look for the all-encompassing statements.

Here are a few examples:

- Successful people don't spend enough time with their families.
- More success brings more freedom.
- Work is difficult.
- Everything is a priority.
- I know what deeply matters to me and I do that.
- My dreams are not practical.
- My dreams are achievable.
- I have to please my parents, lover, spouse, children.
- In living a life I love, I will be better able to support the ones I love.
- I have to know what will happen before I can begin.
- Change is scary.
- I can step into uncertainty with trust and confidence.

What do you believe about living a life you love? Set a timer for 10 minutes and write until it stops.

Beliefs are created through repeated thoughts and experiences. They are not fundamentally or objectively true; they are true because you have consciously or unconsciously decided they are.

Examine each one of the beliefs and labels you carry. Are these the words you want to define your life?

Review and Release. Where did these labels and beliefs come from? Who do they belong to? Set a timer for 10 minutes and write until it stops.

What themes are embedded in the labels and beliefs you wrote? A few thematic examples include: not enough, fearful, trusting, people-pleasing, loving, angry, authentic, sounds like my mom.

Go back through the three life design processes you just completed. Review the labels and beliefs. Question everything, including the labels, personal beliefs, cultural norms, social expectations, political assumptions, and religious ideologies. Be open to release the titles and roles you've gathered throughout your life.

This process takes time and requires you to have compassion for yourself, but it is worth every moment.

Turn these questions over in your mind. If the answers inspire you to release a label or belief, put a line through it.

- Does this label allow you to connect with who you are at your deepest levels?
- Does it allow you to acknowledge all aspects of yourself?
- Is the label or belief working for you?
- Does it help you to feel whole and fulfilled?
- Would you give this label or belief to your child or a loved one?
- You've done a lot of living, learning and growing. Does the label still apply, right now, in this moment?
- What purpose does it serve? To keep you safe? To avoid conflict? To make you right? To keep you connected to your family? To support you in living a life you love?
- What is this label or belief trying to protect you from?
- Does it open you up to the possibilities of life?
- Does it limit you?

- Does it describe your true self?
- Does it describe your constructed self?
- Does it make you afraid?
- Does it keep you open?
- Does it repress you?
- Does it make you happy?
- Does it close you down?
- Do you feel expansive or contracted when you read it?
- Does it allow you to experience your full potential?
- Does it allow you to love yourself and others?
- Does it weigh you down?

- Does it make you feel light?
- Is it liberating?
- Is it imprisoning?
- Does it allow you to experience gratitude?
- Does it support healthy, loving relationships?
- Does it prevent you from experiencing life the way you want to experience it?
- Does it empower you?
- Does it allow you to express yourself?
- Does it allow you to be who you are?

Let it burn.

Use your fireplace, a bonfire, or use a candle if you must. Burn everything that needs to go. Your great life is a Phoenix.

It's time to rise.

delete
enter
return
shift

PART TWO

DESIGN

There is nothing like a
dream to create the future.

VICTOR HUGO

CHAPTER EIGHT

CHANGE YOUR MIND, CHANGE YOUR LIFE

It is not revolutions and upheavals
that clear the road to better days,
but revelations, and lavishness of
someone's soul inspired, and ablaze.

BORIS PASTERNAK

IT IS A TRAVESTY TO BELIEVE THINGS ARE JUST THE WAY THEY ARE; THAT WE ARE without choice, and unable to make changes. When we believe the life that was given to us by our culture, teachers, parents, or friends is the only design we are allowed to use, we suffer. You get to use the life design that works for you. You may have to revolutionize your life, or you may simply have to refine it. Either way, designing a life you love means you are free to reflect on why you think the way you think, why you act the way you act, and to make the changes you want to make.

You get to show up as your unbridled true self, if you choose to. If you are hungry to experience a deeper connection with others and a more grounded sense of self, that's your call. If you think the status quo is broken, you are free to opt out. Alternatively, if the status quo works for you, know that you are free to consciously opt in.

Make the change. If it's authentic, it's all good. Be yourself, you are multi-dimensional, complex, and at times complicated. You may even contradict yourself. As Walt Whitman says, "Do I contradict myself? Very well, then I contradict myself. I am large. I contain multitudes." It's better to design your life and honor the crackled kaleidoscope of your soul than to attempt to embody an inauthentic version of who you think you should be.

What all of this really means is, **you will change.** Often. Change is an important topic in life design. Some folks love change and some folks resist it. What works? What doesn't? How can we lean into creating meaningful, enduring change – not the kind of change that lasts three-and-a-half days?

I've been fascinated by the psychology of change for most of my career. The conditions that create transformative action, goal attainment, and dream nurturance have been studied rigorously. In writing this book, I have been neck-deep in the most effective tools and techniques for making meaningful change and making it last.

Richard Wiseman studied the failure rate of New Year's resolutions and found that 88% of people who set these resolutions fail. Obviously, change can be hard, but there are ways to make it easier. Think of your life design as an evolution instead of a resolution.

If you're resisting it, remember that change is the basis of the universe. The seasons change. The stars change. We change and grow and age. Change is in our DNA. And yet, as a society, we are generally afraid of change. We cover up medical breakthroughs because they contradict what we thought we knew, it takes 15 years for innovative science to replace old facts, we get married when our feelings have changed because we agreed to be engaged, we graduate with degrees we don't want because we started them, and we stay in jobs we hate because we signed a contract.

There are specific strategies that make change stick. These strategies have been infused throughout this book and while I won't blatantly call them out or say, "hey, this is a psychology of change strategy!" please know they are woven into all of the work you do.

* * *

When we revisit Mabel's story and rewind to earlier in her life, we learn how she felt like she was walking through life with her eyes closed. She chose safe office administration jobs and applied her skills to climb the corporate ladder. Deep inside, she always felt like there was something more than her routine of waking up, getting on the bus, going to work, coming home, watching TV, going to sleep, and hitting repeat the next day. "One day, my eyes opened," says Mabel. "I decided I was making a change. I set a date and at a team meeting announced I would be leaving." Mabel was worried about what would happen and the impact it would have on her life. She didn't expect the reaction she got from her boss. After the meeting, he passed her a note that read: *As much as I love having you here, (and I do, I do) I promise to push you out the door if your resolve fails, because it's time you spread your wings.*

The following year, Mabel left her corporate job for an organic farming apprenticeship on Salt Spring Island. This isn't where the story ends. This wasn't her happily ever after. Mabel left the apprenticeship before she completed it. "Even though I didn't finish the program," she says, "I'm so glad I went. Making the decision to do something different changed the course of my life. You don't need to know exactly what you're going to do. Just try it. If it doesn't work out, nothing is set in stone. Just get curious about what's next and start talking about what you're up to with the people you trust. You never know when the next great opportunity will show up in your life."

* * *

When you find yourself investing your time, energy, and attention in places that no longer nourish and energize you, it's time for a change. As you learn, grow, and evolve you will re-chart your course many times. You weren't off track. You just changed. Living a life you love requires constant realignment. Let things fall apart. Embrace the mess. It is fear that says changing your mind is a sign of weakness. It is fear that says changing your mind means you've failed. Fear is a liar, most of the time.

These are not failures: moving across the country for a job and moving back when you realize the job wasn't right for you; switching your degree when your interests change; committing to atheism and then becoming a spiritual guru; starting a business, realizing it's not your thing and shutting it down; saying goodbye when the relationship is no longer in alignment, even if you signed a contract; being a steadfast vegetarian and then eating meat at your best friend's birthday; staying when you said you would leave; saying no after you said yes; saying yes after you said no.

Healing comes when we identify soulful truth and embody the courage to make changes based on what deeply matters. What was interesting to you 10 years ago may not be interesting now. You have permission to change your mind.

When you are facing a crossroads, allow your mind to adventure down both paths. Which feels more truthful?

Which honors what deeply matters to you?

In order to steer steadily through this transition I will remember ...

The next step I will take is ...

What is right for you in this moment
may change in the next.

Allowing fear to make you wrong about
making changes and following your truth
causes unnecessary struggle.

Conscious living is not for the faint of heart.
Take the first step even if you don't know
where the path will lead.

Be brave. Follow your truth. Change your mind.

If I were going to make one change in my life, it would be ...

This change is soulful because ...

Miracles don't happen. You make them happen. They're not wishes or dreams or candles on a cake. They're not impossible. Reality is real. It's totally and completely under my control.

JULIE ANNE PETERS

Repeat after me: *I believe in miracles.* How does it feel? What comes up for you? Miracles happen when we move away from fear, clear out doubt, and challenge unconscious limitations. Having a miracle mindset will allow you to see a future filled with positive possibilities. It will switch you from a "yeah, but" response to a "what if" attitude to living a life you love. Once you're in a "what if" mindset, living a life you love becomes a reality you can more easily embrace.

Steve de Shazer, one of the pioneers of solution focused therapy, created one of my favorite therapy strategies called The Miracle Question. It's my go-to life design technique, because it lights up new neural pathways and stimulates a sense of satisfaction.

Unlike many other psychological strategies, The Miracle Question is a future-oriented, goal-directed strategy rather than a past-oriented, problem-focused strategy. It's a tool to spark creative clarity and define a path for your great life.

The question goes something like this: *Suppose tonight, while you slept, a miracle occurred. When you wake up tomorrow morning your life is exactly the way you want it to be. Walk me through your day and tell me how your life is different. What's better? What kinds of things do you see? How are you thinking and feeling? What is your life like?*

This line of questing can catapult your cognition into a state of creative freedom. The coolest part about The Miracle Question is that your answers reveal pathways for action. You can map out a way to make your miracle, your reality.

Want to wake up in the morning and jump out of bed feeling light, free, and ready for the day? That's totally do-able. We can map out how to get into that state – and it might include more green juice, fewer late nights, more purpose in your work, unsubscribing from stuff that fills up the inbox, turning off reality TV, watching a YouTube video that makes you laugh on your coffee break, or sticking your hands in the river once a week. The Miracle Question opens up possibility and maps out strategy.

Suppose tonight, while you slept, a miracle occurred. When you wake up tomorrow morning your life is exactly the way you want it to be. Walk me through your day and tell me how your life is different. What's better? With your newfound feeling of freedom, what is your life like?

Without the things that have been weighing you down, how do you feel?

Where do you live? Describe your home.

Who are your friends? What is your relationship with them like?

What do you think about?

What kinds of feelings do you have throughout the day?

What is your relationship like with yourself? How do you care for yourself?

Do you have a romantic relationship? Describe it.

How do you give to others? What impact do you have on the world?

How do you care for your body?

What kind of work are you doing? Why does it matter to you?

What are you learning about?

What routines do you engage in?

How do you feel when you go to sleep?

If I were going to make one change in my life, it would be ...

CHAPTER NINE

CORE VALUES AND PRESENT VALUES

Don't ask what the world needs. Ask what makes you come alive and do that. Because what the world needs are people who have come alive.

HOWARD THURMAN

The life you love is built on your core values. Understanding what you value and aligning how you live, love, parent, relate, and work with those values brings a sense of purpose, meaning, and fulfillment to life. When we learn how to identify the things that matter to us, we add richness to our lives.

If you don't uncover your values, you end up defaulting into what other people want, your parent's expectations, or the dominant values of your culture. When we build our lives on the values of others, we allow them to choose what we live for. We become more vulnerable to feeling confused, depressed, unfulfilled, and discontent.

This life design process helps you to clarify your values. Take a look at the following list of values and mark the ones that resonate with you. As you scan the list, you may find that many of the values have little or no significance to you, some may seem negative, and some will resonate deeply.

Review the list of values and put a star next to the values that resonate with you the most.

If you read the value and feel strongly that it's part of who you are and what deeply matters to you, chances are good that it's one of your core values.

Keep in mind we're aiming for 5 core values.

Abundance
Acceptance
Accessibility
Accomplishment
Accuracy
Achievement
Acknowledgement
Activeness
Adaptability
Adoration
Adventure
Affection
Affluence
Aggressiveness
Agility
Alertness
Altruism
Ambition
Amusement
Anticipation
Appreciation
Approachability
Articulacy
Assertiveness
Assurance
Attentiveness
Attractiveness
Audacity
Availability
Awareness
Awe
Balance
Beauty
Being the best
Belonging
Benevolence
Bliss
Boldness
Bravery
Brilliance
Calmness
Camaraderie
Candor
Capability
Care
Carefulness
Celebrity
Certainty
Challenge
Charity
Charm
Chastity
Cheerfulness
Clarity
Cleanliness
Clear-mindedness
Cleverness
Closeness
Comfort
Commitment
Compassion
Completion
Composure
Concentration
Confidence
Conformity
Congruency
Connection
Consciousness
Consistency
Contentment
Continuity
Contribution
Control
Conviction
Conviviality
Coolness
Cooperation
Correctness
Courage
Courtesy
Craftiness
Creativity
Credibility
Cunning
Curiosity
Daring

Decisiveness
Delight
Dependability
Depth
Desire
Determination
Devotion
Dignity
Diligence
Direction
Directness
Discipline
Discovery
Discretion
Diversity
Dreaming
Drive
Duty
Eagerness
Economy
Education
Effectiveness
Efficiency
Elation
Elegance
Empathy
Encouragement
Endurance
Energy
Enjoyment
Entertainment
Enthusiasm
Excellence
Excitement
Exhilaration
Experience
Expertise
Exploration
Expressiveness
Extravagance
Extroversion
Exuberance
Fairness
Faith
Fame
Family
Fascination
Fashion
Fearlessness
Ferocity
Fidelity
Fierceness
Financial independence
Fitness
Flexibility
Flow
Fluency
Focus
Fortitude
Frankness
Freedom
Friendliness
Frugality
Fun
Generosity
Giving
Grace
Gratitude
Gregariousness
Growth
Guidance
Happiness
Harmony
Health
Heart
Helpfulness
Heroism
Holiness
Honesty
Honor
Hopefulness
Hospitality
Humility
Humor
Hygiene
Imagination
Impact

Independence
Ingenuity
Inquisitiveness
Insightfulness
Inspiration
Integrity
Intelligence
Intensity
Intimacy
Introversion
Intuition
Intuitiveness
Inventiveness
Joy
Justice
Keenness
Kindness
Knowledge
Leadership
Learning
Liberation
Liberty
Liveliness
Logic
Longevity
Love
Loyalty
Making a difference
Mastery
Maturity
Meekness
Mellowness
Meticulousness
Mindfulness
Modesty
Motivation
Mysteriousness
Neatness
Nerve
Obedience
Open-mindedness
Openness
Optimism
Order
Organization
Originality
Outrageousness
Peace
Perceptiveness
Perfection
Perseverance
Persistence
Persuasiveness
Passion
Philanthropy
Playfulness
Pleasantness
Pleasure
Poise
Popularity
Potency
Power
Practicality
Pragmatism
Precision
Preparedness
Presence
Privacy
Proactivity
Professionalism
Prosperity
Prudence
Punctuality
Purity
Realism
Reason
Reasonableness
Recognition
Recreation
Refinement
Reflection
Relaxation
Reliability
Religiousness
Resilience
Resolution
Resolve

- Resourcefulness
- Respect
- Rest
- Restraint
- Richness
- Rigor
- Sacredness
- Sacrifice
- Saintliness
- Satisfaction
- Security
- Self-control
- Selflessness
- Self-reliance
- Sensitivity
- Sensuality
- Serenity
- Service
- Sexuality
- Sharing
- Shrewdness
- Significance
- Silence
- Silliness
- Simplicity
- Sincerity
- Skillfulness
- Solidarity
- Solitude
- Speed
- Spirituality
- Spontaneity
- Spunk
- Stability
- Stillness
- Strength
- Structure
- Success
- Support
- Surprise
- Sympathy
- Synergy
- Teamwork
- Thankfulness
- Thoroughness
- Thoughtfulness
- Thrift
- Tidiness
- Timeliness
- Traditionalism
- Tranquility
- Transcendence
- Trust
- Trustworthiness
- Truth
- Understanding
- Uniqueness
- Unity
- Usefulness
- Valor
- Variety
- Victory
- Vigor
- Virtue
- Vision
- Vitality
- Vivacity
- Warmth
- Watchfulness
- Wealth
- Willfulness
- Willingness
- Winning
- Wisdom
- Wittiness
- Wonder
- Youthfulness
- Zeal

KNOWING CORE VALUES

Knowing your core values is the difference between drifting through life, being tossed about by the will of others, and living with clarity, certainty, and confidence.

Defining and knowing your core values gives you a sense of purpose. When you don't know your core values, you'll make most decisions according to circumstances, others' expectations, or pressures from the status quo.

Write down the five values that are most important to you.

My Five Core Values

1. ______________________________
2. ______________________________
3. ______________________________
4. ______________________________
5. ______________________________

Now, rearrange your values in order of priority, placing the most important value at the top.

My Five Core Values in Order

1. ______________________________
2. ______________________________
3. ______________________________
4. ______________________________
5. ______________________________

- Why do you value what you value? Scan your five core values and ask yourself *why?*

- Do they feel like the responsible and mature choices?

- Is it because your lover will appreciate you more?

- Is it because your father disapproves of your decisions?

- It is it because you're rebelling against a set of rules?

- Is it because the thought of living without it makes your soul sad?

- Because you know it's necessary in order to feel alive?

- Is it because you're afraid of the unknown?

- Have you always valued it?

Add some thoughts, feelings, reflection, logic, and understanding into why you value what you value.

When you know your core values, you are less likely to make choices that lead to struggle, "stuckness," and suffering. Your core values are your safety net. If you're feeling overwhelmed or confused about how to live your life, you can fall back on your values. When you encounter a situation and you're unsure of how to handle it, ask yourself, *if I react this way, am I living in alignment with my values?* If the answer is no, I humbly suggest you find a more aligned response.

We all arrive on this planet with possibility and potential – and in order to tap into it, we must know what deeply matters to us. A life lived without a clear understanding of what's most important is a waste of time. And we don't have time to waste.

* * *

When Marc Geronimo went through the core values process, one value floated high above the others – impact. He awakened to the truth that he wanted to have a profound impact on the world. Marc noticed there was a gap between his core values and his present values. Even though he wanted to have a tremendous impact on the world, he avoided taking action in order to live an impactful life.

When Marc reflected on his life and how his value of impact had been neglected, he realized he was afraid of rejection. Marc was valuing security over impact. "I figured out that I hadn't been honoring my value of impact because I wanted to be loved by the people who loved me," says Marc. "I believed if I made a drastic change in my life, I would be putting that love at risk. I was afraid of rejection. I was afraid to be seen in a new light. I was afraid of losing love."

Through the life design process, Marc became aware of a deeper lesson: by building his life from his constructed self instead of his true self, he had lost self-love and self-trust. When he realigned with his core values and focused on cultivating self-love and self-trust, the fear of rejection had less control over him. "Understanding my core values, seeing how I haven't lived them, and knowing how important they are to me has given me the motivation and clarity to resolve this once and for all," says Marc. "It's only been six months and I am 90 percent of the way there, thanks to the life design process!"

* * *

As Marc's experience illustrates, when we are not in love with our life, it's often because our present values don't match our core values. Use this next process to explore whether there is a gap between your core values and your present values.

How are you currently spending your time, money and energy?

Currently, what do you find yourself thinking about the most?

Currently, what do you find yourself talking about the most?

Currently, what do you find yourself doing the most?

How are you practicing your core values?

How are you not practicing your core values?

Reflect on your answers and go back through the list of values – this time marking the values that currently occupy most of your time, money, energy, and attention.

My Five Present Values

1. ______________________________

2. ______________________________

3. ______________________________

4. ______________________________

5. ______________________________

How do your present values differ from your core values?

What needs to change in your thinking, feeling, or behaving so you are embodying your core values on a daily basis?

When you have drifted from your core values, the space between your present life and the life you love can feel massive.

The gap can fill up with frustration, resentment, unhappiness, depression, anxiety, fear, discontent, addiction, loneliness, and boredom.

Too much time away from the home of your soul leads to all kinds of homesickness.

YOUR LIFE DESIGN MANIFESTO

> You were put on this earth to achieve your greatest self, to live out your purpose, and to do it courageously.
>
> **STEVE MARABOLI**

If we follow the meaning of manifesto back to its Latin roots, we find the word *manifestum*, which means clear. You manifesto is a clear declaration of your life. It is grounded in intention and easily anchors you into your core values. It may be bold, outrageous, gritty or gentle.

Your manifesto is the compass that will point you in the direction of a life you love, even when you feel lost. It will embolden your commitment to yourself and your great life. It will provoke authentic change, remind you of your priorities, and align you with the life your soul wants to live.

You may read your manifesto every day, tape it onto your fridge, tuck it into your journal, or have it tattooed onto your skin. Your manifesto isn't necessarily something you declare to the world, though you might. Your manifesto is a medium that leads you to your bright future. It will remind you of your soul's truth, connect you to your core values, encourage mindfulness, and guide your purposeful decision-making.

While there is no right or wrong way to write a manifesto, I encourage you to choose words that represent how you want to be and what you want to do.

The manifesto that guides my life as I'm writing this book is ...

Live freely.
Love deeply.
Explore wildly.

The *doing* component of my manifesto is live, love, and explore.
The *being* component of my manifesto is free, deep, and wild.

* * *

After Melsha Shea designed her life, she became aware of how her weight was preventing her from living a life she loved. She didn't go whitewater rafting because she was worried she wouldn't fit into the wet suit, she was hiding in baggy, plus-sized clothes, and she longed to climb a mountain.

Melsha realized that living a life she loved meant being fit and healthy, so she could do anything her heart desired. She designed her life and felt called to share her real, raw, and vulnerable life design story with others.

Melsha started a blog with her manifesto emblazoned across the top of the website: authentically me, perfectly imperfect. Her first post made a splash on the Internet as she revealed her bikini pictures and made a declaration of self-love. Melsha's manifesto keeps her connected to what matters and gives her the strength to show up with vulnerability, courage, and gratitude.

* * *

Your manifesto is your process for making powerful choices. When your life becomes your manifesto, you become connected to your true self, you feel at home in your life, you walk tall, think clearly, and live purposefully. What do you believe about living a life you love?

It's helpful for your manifesto to include words that describe the essence of the life you want to live. These words will feel inherent, natural, essential, fundamental, and core. Often, these are the being words. They describe what you are. Your being words will represent the overall feeling of your life, and they will speak to the big things that deeply matter.

We also need to balance being with doing, because too much being can lead to stagnation. If we don't balance being with doing, we bypass living. Therefore, it is also important to include doing words in your manifesto. This is your life in movement, flow, and action. The doing is the expression of your being. It represents the evolution of your life and the gifts you give the world. Beware – too much doing leads to burnout, overwhelm, and exhaustion. First, commit to how you want to be, then decide what you will do.

Your manifesto is the distilment of your life design. It is the essence of who you are, what matters to you and the life you want to live. It's a reflection of what you know to be true. Words are powerful; they carry energy, intention, and momentum. Your manifesto will represent the design of your life, the truth of your soul, the intention in your action, and the clarity with which you move through the world.

* * *

Tanya Geisler had a successful career in advertising. She logged long hours, took excellent care of her clients and reaped the rewards. But she craved a different kind of reward – a sense of delight in her work and joy in her existence. It was only after her mother's death that she really heard her mother's mantra: *Don't postpone joy.* Tanya's soul searching began. She switched careers, excavated her values, and lived by a word: Joy. "Step into your most glorious, radiant, productive, purposeful self," says Tanya. "Use your life and your gifts to instigate change and instill joy. Do it for yourself and the world."

* * *

Your manifesto may be one word, like Tanya's, a sentence like Melsha's or a collection of statements like mine. There is no correct way to create your life design manifesto, but here are a few guidelines.

Make it personal. What are the words that speak to your soul? The lines of poetry that make you relax into life? The quotes that light your fire? Your manifesto is written for you and you alone. You may, of course, share it with others, but what matters most is that you know why it's meaningful.

Be accurate. Language is layered and rich. Clichés can be authentic, but they can also be limiting. Your manifesto will be nuanced and distinctive. Study the definition and the meaning of the words that resonate with you.

Be expansive. There may be words from other cultures or languages that capture the essence of what matters to you. Your soul has no nation. Explore the world.

Honor your soul. Your life design manifesto is the expression of soulful embodiment. It's the living document that aligns your mind, body, spirit, and life. It's what allows you to remember the truth of who you are when the going gets tough.

Base it on liberation and love. In the past you may have felt fearful, trapped, or out of sync with your true self. Your manifesto represents your sovereign reign over the life you love.

What life design words and concepts feel most important to you?

I am living my great life when ...

What galvanizes you? What inspires you? Distill the essence of the life you love into a few words.

CHAPTER TEN

DESIGN YOUR BLUEPRINT

Your soul knows the geography of
your destiny better than you do.

JOHN O'DONOHUE

THERE ARE VARIOUS WAYS TO DESCRIBE THE COMPLEX WEB OF MYSTERY called neural pathways. I call neural pathways "blueprints" because they show us how to build our lives.

In order to build a life we love, we must design a great blueprint. A blueprint is a collection of beliefs, values, behaviors, preferences, patterns, and thoughts. *Do this. Value that. Want these things. Think like this. Avoid him. Pursue her. Eat this. Wear that. Feel this. Say that.*

The more often you think, feel, or behave in a certain way, the more you create a blueprint that matches that way of being. The more you use a particular blueprint, the stronger and faster it becomes, which means the most frequently used blueprints become your dominant way of living.

Your blueprints become part of you and guide how you think, feel, and behave. You have blueprints for everything in your life: how to drive, how you like your coffee, how you deal with conflict, what kind of books you like to read, the work you want to do in the world, who you are attracted to, how you spend your money, how you deal with stress... and the list goes on.

Your senses gather roughly 11 million bits of information per second and send them to the brain for processing, but the conscious mind can only process about 50 bits per second. What is processed and what is filtered depends largely on the blueprints that are running in your mind. When you change your blueprints, you change your perception, and you change your life.

Many of our blueprints are created early in life. As children, we are taught what to believe, what to think, who we are, how life works, and what kind of world we live in. We inherit our blueprints from our mothers, fathers, teachers, coaches, and any other influential role models in our young lives. When we are young, the blueprints of others dictate our lives; they control how we navigate the world around us and how we survive.

Sometimes, others' blueprints serve us well. Often they do not. As adults, our minds are filled with dead ideas and lifeless beliefs that do not belong to us. They are burdensome, yet we cling to them because we haven't designed our own blueprints. Old patterns remain our default until we create a new set of fresh blueprints for ourselves.

If the blueprint theory feels depressingly deterministic, please know your conscious choice is more powerful than your outdated blueprints. You can design the blueprints from which you want to build your life.

We came here to live our true lives, not the lives that our parents, teachers, partners or friends want us to live. In order to direct our lives, we must consciously design our own blueprints. Do your blueprints support you in living a life you love? Simply by asking this question, you open space in your mind to create more authentic blueprints.

Designing your great life is a matter of decoding your soul's desires and creating a design that your heart can trust and your mind can follow.

We all have a collection of conscious and unconscious blueprints. The dominant, conscious blueprint is to go to school, get a job, find love, buy a house, have kids. We're all aware of the basic life plan our culture tries to siphon us into. The unconscious blueprints are less obvious and they are different for each of us.

Here are some common refrains I hear in my practice:

> *It's not safe to be my true self because I might be rejected.*
>
> *I don't deserve to have ... (love, success, abundance, attention, respect).*
>
> *I'm not (good, beautiful, smart, sexy, rich, thin, successful, strong) enough.*
>
> *I must sacrifice my desires to make others happy and gain their approval.*
>
> *In order to be successful, I must be ... (educated, younger, older, smarter).*
>
> *I'll be happy when ... (my kids listen to me, my husband changes, my boss respects me, I get the promotion, I lose the weight).*

There have been dozens of times in my life when I have suddenly become aware of an outdated blueprint. Sometimes it's amusing, sometimes it's enlightening, sometimes it completely shatters my world. But in the shards, a more accurate and meaningful blueprint can emerge.

The discomfort of creating new blueprints can be extreme. The confusion of redefining your existence can be profound. The uncertainty of what's truthful can be paralyzing. The ache to return to the comfortable and familiar is an enticing pull, but following it will only prolong suffering. As uncomfortable as it is, bursting into your new world, complete with new blueprints, is the most soulfully satisfying action that you can take.

Settle in and draft your new blueprint. Pay attention and listen to your soul. Notice your instincts and follow them. Let your true self take the lead. Be open to redefining everything you thought you knew.

- How would it feel to be living a life I love?
- What would I be thinking about if I were living a life I love?
- How would I be acting if I were living a life I love?
- What do I choose to believe about myself in order to live a life I love?
- What do I choose to believe about others in order to live a life I love?
- What do I choose to believe about the world in order to live a life I love?

MAKE YOUR MARK

It's time to get out of your head and get closer to your heart. Writing is a cognitive process, so to access your heart, it's time to spark up your creativity.

Find some colorful writing instruments, like crayons, markers, paints, Jiffys – whatever you have nearby. If you want to scour magazines for inspiring images to rip out and paste on your blueprint, go for it!

Get crafty! Draw, collage, paint. Claim your blueprint. Make your mark.

What are the images that come to mind? Find them or draw them and stick them on your blueprint.

What colors represent the life that is calling to you?

What are the images that come to mind? Find them or draw them and stick them on your blueprint.

What does it smell like?

What symbols represent the blueprint of your life design?

If you suspect that you have a persistent, unwanted blueprint you just can't shake, connect with your favorite psychologist. Most shrinks are trained to help you heal past injuries, process deeply-held limiting beliefs, integrate incomplete stages of development, and smash the unconscious barriers that keep you stuck.

As you begin to develop your blueprints based on what your soul wants – not your culture, your family, or your ego – you step courageously and confidently in the direction of living a life you love. Your blueprint may change the course of your career, it may lead to a soulful community, a deeper relationship with yourself, an awakening, an ending, a beginning. It could change your life for the better or start a revolution. It could inspire a new way to pay the rent or spark a wild adventure.

Before you live your life from the blueprint you just created, ask yourself. Do I want this blueprint to guide my life?

Does this blueprint make me feel energized or burdened?

Do I feel relief?

Do I feel appreciative and grateful?

Does this feel like the life I want to come home to?

Is this an accurate description of the life my soul wants to live?

Can I grow into this life?

Does this life make me feel expansive?

NEGOTIATION

> May the forms of your belonging - in love, creativity and friendship be equal to the grandeur and the call of your soul.
>
> JOHN O'DONOHUE

When you are designing a life you love, there will be a period of negotiation before you take action. Negotiation takes place as you tune into your soul's desire and discern what your heart and mind are ready to do. Negotiation also happens as you move away from your real life, into your ideal life, and navigate the relationships that will be affected by your life design.

Much like designing a custom home, it's important to reflect on what kind of design process feels right for you. Will you demolish and construct in a flurry? Will you slowly and thoughtfully take down piece-by-piece and rebuild? Are minor tweaks necessary? Does your life need a deep renovation from tiptop to bedrock bottom? Will you roll up your sleeves and do most of the work yourself? Or will you call on experienced and skilled people to guide you along the way?

If you feel indecisive, remember you can change your mind. Begin by committing to a process, take some small steps, and engage in conscious reflection.

Living a life you love has to be sustainable. Consider what resources you have available to you right now. This isn't a race; there is no finish line. You set the pace and you can speed it up or slow it down as needed.

DREAM

Dreaming, imagining, and envisioning your future is critical for life design. Of course, there is tremendous value in living in the present. When we are present, we are more able to express gratitude, cultivate healthy relationships, express our creativity, and reduce stress. All good things.

Dreaming of the life you love doesn't betray the life you have. You can be fully in, and grateful for, the life you have while desiring something different in the future.

Think of someone you know who is living a great life. Their life isn't perfect, but they know who they are and they are clear about the life they want to live. When they get off track, they make changes and find their way back to the life they love. Write down some words to describe this person.

When you imagine living a life you love, how would you describe it?

These qualities may be different than the ones you just wrote down. Feel the life you are meant to be living, the life that has been calling to you, the life your soul aches to love. Write the words that come to you. Look at the words you have written. How are these qualities missing in your life?

How are these qualities already in your life, even in a small way?

What do you really love about your life and why?

It's time to juggle. Hold everything you've read in this book in your mind as you envision your future. What's the vision for a soulful life you love five years from now? Write it out.

When you are dreaming you are not committing. Rather, you are creating tension. When you hold the soulful vision of your future, you create tension between life as it is right now and the life you love. You are creating momentum between what is and what can be. This tension is the creative force that will pull you into your future. If we don't hold a vision of the future, we don't have the energy required to move into something new and we stay stuck where we are.

There are two ways to relieve the tension. You can release the vision of living a life you love and settle back into the way things are, or you can move from the way things are into the soulful way you want them to be.

Will you choose the status quo or your soul?

CHAPTER ELEVEN

ANNUAL SOUL PLAN

None of us will ever accomplish anything excellent or commanding except when he listens to this whisper, which is heard by him alone.

RALPH WALDO EMERSON

PURSUE YOUR DREAM FOR THE SAKE OF YOUR SOUL, NOT FOR APPROVAL, acceptance or accolades. Climb the mountain to see the world, not so the world can see you. Travel to 100 countries not to cross them off your list and show your friends how worldly you are, but to experience 100 countries. Write a song, not for applause, but for the harmony it will bring to your life. Stay at home to take care of your family not because you want to be a good parent, but because the thought of choosing something different makes your soul sad.

Your annual soul plan is built from what deeply matters and it is aligned with your core values. Your soul plan begins with intention and flows into action.

INTENTION

Your intention is a focus point to help you find your way when you're feeling lost and a keystone to create connection when you feel disconnected. It will help you choose to be in service of your soul rather than a slave to your ego. Your intention is a question or a statement formed around what you most want in your life.

Before you set your intention, connect with your deepest desires. Danielle LaPorte, creator of *The Desire Map* asks, "what if, first, we got clear on how we actually wanted to feel in our life, and then we laid out our intentions? What if your most desired feelings consciously informed how you plan your day, your year, your career, your holidays – your life?" Form your intention around your deepest desires and, if you're wondering what you desire, get *The Desire Map*. Once you've connected to what you desire, settle into yourself, and reflect on how you want to create intention.

Your intention can be structured as a statement or a question. Intention statements tend to be solid, steady, and create structure. Intention questions tend to open us up to possibility, wonder, and curiosity. It's the difference between, *this year, I intend to ask myself how I might add more adventure into my life.* And, *this year I intend to be more adventurous.* Which one feels better to you? There is no right answer. There is only your answer.

Once you have decided whether to structure your intention as a question or a statement, it's time to connect to your soul. If you're a meditator, slip into meditation. If you're not a meditator, take a few deep breaths and let your awareness sink from your mind down into your body. What do you most want this year? How do you want to feel? What do you want to experience? What intentions would you like to set in each area of your life?

Your intentions may direct you toward a bigger, brighter life. Or, they may suggest a slower, simpler life. Reflect on all the work you've already done in this book and set intentions that originate from your true self instead of your constructed self. The dominant forces in our culture often push us toward becoming richer, sexier, and happier. Be aware of what is influencing your intention. How does it feel to want what you want? Does it feel forced and fake? Does it feel aligned and true? Does it feel commercial and contrived? Does it feel authentic and pure?

If you'd like to set your intentions immediately, skip ahead a few pages to write them out. Be sure to come back, though, because we have plenty more to cover. Alternatively, you may choose to allow your intentions to float in your mind before committing them to paper. If that's the case, please, continue.

Once you have set your intentions, it's time to create actions to support your intentions.

ACTIONS

The action section of your annual soul plan must be self-reliant and self-referencing. In order to live a life you love, it's important to consciously reflect on how you want to be (intention) and what you want to do (action). Above all, your doing must be soulful.

Soulful actions will sound something like this: *I'm going to start my day off with a 10-minute walk outside because my soul wants to move my body and feel connected to nature.*

When our actions are based in ego, or the constructed self, we quickly burn out. Egoic plans are difficult to maintain and often lead to struggle and self-sabotage. *An egoic plan will sound more like this: I'm going to start my day off with a 10-minute walk outside because that fitness magazine said it would boost my metabolism, I'd lose weight, impress my boyfriend, and finally fit into my skinny jeans.*

Your *why* is your billion-dollar question. Why do you want what you want? Before you commit to your soulful actions, approach them with curiosity and openness. Being curious and open creates space for authentic discernment and allows you to feel the difference between soulful action and egoic action. Developing our ability to be discerning allows us to consistently move toward the life we love by choosing intentions and actions that align with our true self.

Being out of alignment with your true self feels uncomfortable. Making plans based on your constructed self creates struggle, stuckness, and suffering. The constructed self will design a life that feels confining, like walking through life wearing a straightjacket. Even if you have repressed your true self in the past, it is always possible to invite soul back into your life. It is never too late to be yourself. It's never too late to change course. It is never too late to live a life you love.

There are three qualities to soulful actions. One, they have metrics. Two, they are meaningful. Three, they are completely dependent on you.

METRICS

Knowing whether or not you are actually living by your soul plan provides the momentum necessary to continue designing and living a life you love. When choosing your actions for the year, try to add numbers and dates. We want you to be able to easily say, "yes, I did the thing I wanted to do!" While I do encourage you to sync up your intentions with measurable actions, your annual soul plan is open to outcome, not attached to it. We don't want this to become another reason why you beat yourself up or feel like you're not good enough.

MEANING

It's unlikely your true self will measure success according to material accumulation, climbing the promotional ladder, achieving celebrity, completing a project, tucking cash in the bank, or any other egoic evaluation of success. Nor will it measure success by "good things," like how often you practice yoga, how much money you donate to charity, how often you volunteer, whether you hit your meditation pillow every morning, or how many countries you've visited. These tend to be evaluations from the constructed self.

Your soulful definitions of success will feel pure. Your true self is more likely to measure success according to how aligned you are with your values, your sense of meaning, being on purpose, or feeling fulfilled. Your soul may view success as taking one step in the direction of your true self, no matter how light, dark, smooth or messy it is. You may need to stop a project halfway through, quit hot yoga because it gives you a headache, decline the dream job, or cancel the trip. Anything that stifles the soul is on the chopping block, no matter how "good" it seems.

SELF-RELIANCE

Your true self may want to set an intention to explore the world by traveling to one new country per year. Your constructed self may protest: *yes, but I don't think I can do it by myself. I have to get my friend to do it with me.* Your constructed self places this limiting need for a travel companion on your soul plan because it's afraid.

Connect with the actions that feed your soul and can be achieved without depending on other people. This doesn't mean you're completely on your own; you may want others to join you on your sacred adventure, but you are not dependent on them. Though it may be uncomfortable, this frees you, and them, to live a life you love.

* * *

Mel lived in a fast-paced, corporate, results-oriented city, but her soul called her to a slower life. When Mel eased up the pace of her life she felt lazy, self-indulgent, and inadequate. In order to fully step into the life she loved, she needed to opt out of the dominant culture's standards of success and define her own.

Mel started by practicing acceptance and gratitude for what she already had. Then she began evaluating her success based on whether or not she was doing the work her soul wanted to do. "I've known from a young age I am meant to be doing healing work," says Mel. "I've been interested in different healing modalities for as long as I can remember and I've always loved offering help and healing to others. At times in my life I hid my gifts as a healer because it requires I live a slower life, but now I know they need to be shared. When I don't allow my soul's calling to be expressed in the world I feel unsettled, like my life is a sham."

* * *

When building a life you love, you may be called to an annual soul plan that feels big. You might start a new career, sell the house, begin dating again, travel the world. If working 40 hours week in a 9-5 gig feels constricting, change your work. If more than one social activity per day is over-stimulating, take space. If a phone call instead of a text message keeps you feeling connected, make the call. If you need to make your home beautiful to ensure your soul's comfort, beautify it.

On the other hand, you may be called to make smaller shifts. Which books resonate with you? Read those. Which restaurants nourish you on all levels? Eat there. What music allows your soul to settle? Listen to it. Which hobbies allow your soul to thrive? Pursue them.

If it feels like the life you love is miles away, you can set intentions that are closer. Commit to actions that move you from what is real right now to what is ideal in your not-so-distant future. There are many ways to move from what is real to what is ideal in life design. For example, imagine that you go gaga for the ocean. But, you live in the tallest high-rise in a booming metropolis. Real is your high rise and ideal is the thatched roof beach hut your soul craves. Giving up your apartment, quitting your job, and letting your kids raise themselves might feel too drastic or it might even feel offensive. Maintaining your commitments while waking up to the sound of the ocean rolling through your iPhone and nibbling on fresh pineapple slices for breakfast might move you closer to your soul's desire, while respecting what has heart and meaning for your real life.

On the other hand, dreams and plans that seem far away can spark creativity. Want to design a new product? Imagine doing it in Bali. Want to run a marathon? Contemplate what it would be like to run it in the desert. Want to contribute some cash to a meaningful project? Imagine becoming a philanthropic angel investor. Just for fun, try expanding the limits of what you think is possible.

Planning to live a life you love is important, but it is secondary to connecting with the truth of your soul. In order to create momentum and live with soulful metrics, planning matters. As you move through this next process, please remember that self-trust, deep listening, courageous conversations, and sacred action are all part of the plan.

CREATING YOUR ANNUAL SOUL PLAN

Your plan must be scaled to your soul and it must be sustainable. Metrics matter when engaging in life design, but ultimately, if you don't have meaning, your plan doesn't have soul.

As you create your annual soul plan please remember that being is more important than doing. First, check in with how you want to be (your intention) and then choose actions to support your intention.

CATEGORIES

It's helpful to separate out the different areas of life that matter to you. I divide mine up into these categories. You are welcome to use mine or craft your own.

Health – daily routines, food, rest, activity, medications, supplements, practitioners, sexuality, meditation, time in nature, hydration, vacations, cooking, sports.

Stuff – your physical home, art, objects, technology, decor, landscape, tools, possessions, books.

Relationships – connection, conversation, community, belonging, relating, family, friends, co-workers, solitude, celebration, entertaining, socializing.

Growth – personal philosophy, therapy, religion, spirituality, coaching, education, books, workshops, retreats, travel, creative expression, hobbies, interests, devotion.

Work – position, time off, job, promotion, career, profession, credentials, products, services, networking, marketing, deliverables.

Money – earning, bonus, raise, spending, saving, investing, healing your relationship with money, buying.

Giving – philanthropy, being of service, donating, promoting, voting, causes, issues, projects, contribution, volunteering, sponsoring, advising, mentoring, tithing.

I suggest you set at least one intention for each area of life. You are welcome to set more intentions, of course, but I offer a word of caution: If your annual soul plan feels unmanageable and overwhelming, you are more likely to stick it on the shelf and watch it gather dust. When beginning your life design process, start with one intention per category. By focusing on one intention at a time, you are more likely to experience success, and success builds confidence and momentum.

If you are a seasoned life designer, feel free to add more intentions per section. I usually have about three intentions per category that I work on each year. Begin reflecting on your intentions now and we'll write them down in a few pages.

CHOOSING SUPPORTIVE ACTIONS

Once you have your intention, map out the actions required in order to make your intention a reality. If we don't write down what we need to do in order to live the life we love, we have a vision without a plan, and nothing changes. How can you make your annual soul plan actionable and bring it to life?

It can be really helpful to work backwards. Let's pretend you set this intention:

I intend to explore how I can support my community through volunteerism.

Once you've reflected on your intention, let's pretend that volunteering at 10 different organizations throughout the year would be really meaningful. Your backwards breakdown might look like this:

December – volunteer at organization #10
November – volunteer at organization #9
October – volunteer at organization #7 and #8
September – volunteer at organization #5 and # 6
June – volunteer at organization #3 and #4
April – volunteer at organization #1 and #2
March – finalize my commitment to each organization
February – investigate the 10 organizations I will volunteer at
January – create a soulful goal to volunteer at 10 organizations

ACTIONABLE IDEAS

Slap a coat of paint on the walls if periwinkle is more soulful than mauve. Pick up some fresh flowers during your weekly grocery shop to add a dash of life and color to your space. Maybe it's time for a new hair color? Go blue if you want to. Remember that marathon you wanted to run? Start training.

When you gather with your friends, you might suggest heading out for a walk in nature instead of sitting in your local coffee shop. Maybe you buy books at local bookstores instead of shopping on Amazon. You might click over to Etsy and have an artisan personalize a t-shirt, wall art, or a piece of jewelry that reminds you of your life design.

Volunteer for a charitable cause that aligns with your core values. Create a screen saver to remind you of your soulful goals. Design a daily check-in list with your specific action plans mapped out.

During your weekly date night, check in with your partner about how his or her life design is going. Set up a texting buddy system with your life design friends to help keep you on track and remind you all of what matters. Create a playlist with songs that pump you up or settle you down into the life you love. If the design of your life involves more creative expression, swap your lunch location from the restaurant chain to the café in the art gallery.

Your annual soul plan could include honoring your heritage by practicing cultural traditions or it might mean redefining your relationship with the divine – no matter how you were baptized.

After you've established your intention, follow up with supportive actions in order to avoid becoming overwhelmed with the burden of unexecuted ideas.

Here's an example of what a soulful goal and action plan might look like.

Soulful Growth Intention: I intend to reconnect with my passion for culture and adventure by exploring Peru.

Soulful Growth Action

- Say yes to the request to facilitate a retreat in Peru
- Save $150 per month for travel expenses
- Prepare content for the retreat by July
- Update my passport in August
- Book my flight in September
- Find my backpack
- Research the culture and places I want to experience in Peru

In this section, you'll find a series of prompts for each part of your annual soul plan. First you'll engage in reflection, then you'll establish your intention, and finally, you'll flesh out your actions.

SOULFUL HEALTH

daily routines, food, rest, activity, medications, supplements, practitioners, sexuality, meditation, time in nature, hydration, vacations, cooking, sports

- How will you express gratitude for the health you have?
- When I don't get enough rest it's because I ...
- When I avoid caring for my body it's because ...
- When I have pushed myself too hard I feel ...
- What unhealthy habits are you ready to let go of?
- What healthy habits are you ready to incorporate?
- How will you take care of your physical, emotional, and mental health?
- A few different things make me feel energetic, including ...
- If I could choose any form of exercise in the world it would be ...
- I nourish my soul when I ...

Soulful health intention:

Soulful health actions:

SOULFUL STUFF

your physical home, art, objects, technology, decor, landscape, tools, possessions, books

- I long for my home to feel ...
- This year, I want to add these things to my home ...
- Even though it seems outrageous, I really want ...
- In order to add more soul into my relationship with my stuff, I will get rid of ...

Soulful stuff intention:

Soulful stuff actions:

SOULFUL RELATIONSHIPS

connection, conversation, community, belonging, relating, family, friends, co-workers, solitude, entertaining, socializing

- What do you want to do with your loved ones?
- What conversations do you want to have?
- What relational pattern do you want to change?
- How will you connect with your loved ones?
- Who will you spend time with?
- What community do you want to create or be part of?
- How will you support the soulful growth of the people in your life?
- How will you honor the differences of the people you are in relationship with?
- How you will live with courageous integrity within your relationships?
- I am really excited to celebrate my relationships by ...
- I want to be friends with people who ...
- The kind of friend I want to be is ...

Soulful relationship intention:

Soulful relationship actions:

LIFE DESIGN PROCESS: SOULFUL RELATIONSHIP INTENTION AND ACTION

SOULFUL GROWTH

personal philosophy, therapy, religion, spirituality, coaching, education, books, workshops, retreats, travel, creative expression, hobbies, research interests, self-exploration, devotion

- I stop myself from being creative when I ...
- When I am unhappy in my life, it's because ...
- What books do you want to read?
- What workshops do you want to attend?
- What hobbies do you want to explore?
- What place do you want to visit?
- My inner rhythm is ...
- I want to express my creativity by ...
- What do you want to be devoted to?
- I secretly long for ...
- I'd be really happy to experience more ...

Soulful growth intention:

Soulful growth actions:

SOULFUL WORK

position, promotion, time off, profession, credentials, products, raise, services, networking, marketing, deliverables, projects, leave of absence, bonus

- What do you want to achieve in your work this year?
- How specifically will you live your purpose?
- How do you want to 'be' in your work this year?
- How will you earn a living, support yourself, and support those who depend on you?
- What does your soul call you to do for work?
- What do you want to change about your work?

Soulful work intention:

Soulful work actions:

SOULFUL MONEY

earning, spending, saving, investing, working on relationship with money, buying

- What do you want your relationship with money to be like?
- What percentage of your paycheck do you want to go into savings or use to pay off debt?
- How will you spend your money? Feather your nest? Take a trip? Save for a wine cellar?
- What gifts will you give yourself this year?
- Do you want to change your relationship with money? If yes, how?
- What do you really love about your life and why?

Soulful money intention:

Soulful money actions:

SOULFUL GIVING

philanthropy, being of service, donating, promoting, voting, causes, issues, projects, contribution, volunteering, advising, mentoring, tithing

- How do you want to be of service this year?
- Where do you want to volunteer?
- Who do you want to support?
- What organization do you want to donate to?
- What impact do you want to have on others?
- I want to care for the earth by ...
- I would like to serve the world by ...
- The one thing I really want the world to know is ...

Soulful giving intention:

Soulful giving actions:

BRINGING IN

Because you've already begun removing what is not aligned with the life you want to live, you have created space for your life design plan to swing into action.

Every week, bring one thing into your life that supports your annual soul plan – a courageous conversation, an empowering thought, a supportive activity, a sacred ritual, a meaningful object, a new relationship, an expression of gratitude, an interesting hobby, an act of generosity, a kind word when you look at yourself in the mirror.

BRING IT TO LIFE

Soulful intention? Check. Actionable steps? Check. Now, make it beautiful!

Splash some color on your annual soul plan. Collage inspiring images, sew in some fabric, sprinkle some sparkles if that's your thing. Brush some paint on the pages, doodle meaningful symbols throughout; I've kept the design of this book simple so you can make your mark.

Craft your annual soul plan into something you want to enjoy, cherish, and use frequently. And, I do suggest you look at it frequently.

heal the past

CHAPTER TWELVE

CRAFTING SOULFUL RITUALS

The soul requires ritual that meets our deepest needs. Rituals that other people like may not hit the true, innermost parts of us. We can risk doing ritual our own way. In fact, we must.

ROBIN RICE

LIVING CONSCIOUSLY REQUIRES ENERGY, ATTENTION, AND EFFORT, BUT THE conscious mind has a limited capacity to sustain all three of these things. In order to support conscious living, it's helpful to craft rituals that are aligned with the life you love.

Our daily lives are primarily a result of unconscious ways of being and subconscious rituals – the food we eat, the way we talk to our children, whether we pour ourselves a drink at the end of the day or go for a run, how we spend our money, the way we deal with emails, how we feel in relationship, what we think when we look at ourselves in the mirror. More than 40% of the actions we take are based on subconscious rituals.

When we first start creating change, our brain is hyperactive; it has to work hard to make sense of the world as we move through new behavioral territory. With enough repetition, the thinking part of our mind gets quiet and our brain's automatic systems take over.

Our brain is constantly trying to conserve energy, so it will always try to turn behaviors into automatic rituals. It's an excellent process that allows us to evolve and we can use it to design a life we love.

Within our days there are many wasted moments: the minutes between when the alarm rings and when you get out of bed, looking in the closet trying to decide what to wear, sitting at your desk figuring out what work to begin. When harnessed, these wasted moments can add momentum and satisfaction to our lives. Rituals allow us to massage mundane, in-between moments into meaningful experiences.

Rituals are used all over the world, by all kinds of people, in all kinds of ways. While there's tremendous variety in these rituals, they all have one thing in common: people who perform rituals report feeling better about their lives. While rituals are infused into many different religious practices, rituals are not inherently religious. They are created to encode meaningful behavior into life experiences. Regardless of your religious or spiritual beliefs, performing rituals can help you enjoy life and make meaningful changes.

Our world is over-stimulating and, at times, stressful. The media coaxes us into believing we can be happier, healthier, sexier, and more successful if we just consume more stuff. At some level we know the truth, and in order to live a life we love there are changes we need to make. Whether it's in our perceiving, thinking, feeling, or behaving, the only way to experience a different reality is to do something different.

THE MUNDANE AND THE SACRED

When we add the texture of faith, wonder, awe, and reverence into our moments, we are choosing to engage with the sacredness of life. Injecting sacredness into our lives does not mean we are subscribing to, or unsubscribing from, a particular religion. It means we are consciously choosing to add meaning to times, dates, places, and spaces.

When our lives feel flat, empty, or one-dimensional, it is often because we are focused on the mundane and our days lack sacredness. Our lives are infused with humdrum rituals: brushing your teeth, flipping on the TV after work, shaking hands when you meet someone. Most of these rituals were handed down to us by others and often, they work well.

Other rituals stem from obligation or expectation. The commercialization of holidays has us giving cards and gifts because we are supposed to. We end conversations with 'I love you,' but the words can feel automatic and empty. When we establish soulful rituals, we are less likely to engage in mindless consumerism, empty conversations, and ineffective habits. When we consciously choose how we want to live and create rituals to support our intentions, life becomes easier and more enjoyable.

When designing a life you love, you will infuse what is sacred into the mundane. Your sacred rituals will support the soul plan you have created for yourself and can be integrated into every area of life. Managing email, initiating conversations, sipping coffee, going for a run, waking up in the morning, and traveling the world can all be enhanced by establishing rituals, which is the process of creating a default pattern that will work well for you most of the time.

Here are a few examples of life design rituals:

> *"Every morning, when I wake up, I turn on a playlist that helps me ease into the day. Listening to my favorite music first thing in the morning gives me the motivation to get out of bed and sets the tone for the day."*
>
> *"Instead of checking social media throughout the day, I decided to create an online connection time. At 3 pm, I open up my social media networks and check out what everyone is up to. I give myself 30 minutes to indulge in the Internet – in whatever way inspires me – and then I shut it down. I look forward to this time all day and once it's over, I feel satisfied and I'm able to focus on my work."*
>
> *"I used to waste three hours every evening watching television. I realized how unsatisfied I felt, so I created an evening ritual. After my kids go to bed, I read or write until 10 pm. When 10 pm hits, I know it's time for my candlelit bath. I fill the tub with*

steamy water, light my candles, and slide in. Finishing my day off in this way helps me to fall asleep faster and feel good about how I'm spending my evening."

"I've struggled with creating an exercise routine for years. Once I ritualized it, exercise became easier to stick to. Now, when it's my lunch break, I automatically go outside and walk for 30 minutes. After I'm done, I come back and eat my lunch. It's simple, really, but making it a ritual made it so much easier."

"I found I was craving more connection in my life, so I ritualized the way I greet people. I focused on being incredibly present, shaking their hand, and holding it for a few extra seconds while looking into their eyes. I would think to myself, 'I see you' and I would focus on really seeing them. The effect was extraordinary. My conversations were interesting and I quickly developed more meaningful relationships with people."

You can create meaningful rituals in all areas of life, whether it's a family tradition, a cup of tea, or a walk in nature. Above all, rituals are deliberate, intentional, and conscious.

Ingraining a ritual can take time. Establishing a ritual requires conscious attention and focus. Over time, the ritual will drop into your subconscious mind and will become an effortless part of your day.

By consciously infusing our lives with the transformative power of rituals, we can deepen our relationship with our soul, with others, and the world at large.

In what ways do your current rituals already support you?

In what ways do your current rituals not support you?

What rituals do you want to commit to that will support you in living a life you love?

If you were consistent in these rituals for a year, how would your life be different?

80/20 RULE

The Pareto Principle is also known as the 80/20 rule. Its foundation lies in economics and was proven using statistical analysis. While the theory is interesting and worth further investigation, the key piece of information for the purposes of life design is that 20 percent of your activities will produce about 80 percent of the results in your life.

Living a life you love does not result from more striving. It's about doing what matters. Eighty percent of your great life will come from 20 percent of your energy, time, money, and attention.

The 80/20 life design principle can make the daunting task of life design seem less daunting. It's the magic formula that can make your annual soul plan manageable and do-able. It's a powerful equation for solid, soulful action.

You can apply these golden numbers to many areas of life, but we're going to laser in on how creating rituals based on the 80/20 rule can tip you in the direction of living a life you love.

Which 20% of activities support 80% of your happiness and joy?

Which 20% of activities cause 80% of your stress?

Which 20% of your friends contribute to 80% of the fun and love in your life?

Which 20% of your friends contribute to 80% of the drama and dysfunction in your life?

What 20% of your possessions feel most aligned with the life you love?

Which 20% of your work causes 80% of your results?

What 20% of your thoughts create a sense of peace in your life?

Which 20% of the food you eat gives you the most amount of energy and vitality?

What 20% of your clothes do you love wearing and feel great in?

How can you increase the amount of time, money, energy, and attention you invest in the 20% of life that brings you the most peace, happiness, fulfillment, connection, joy, success, and love?

How can you reduce or minimize the amount of time, money, energy, and attention you invest into the 20% of life that causes you stress, frustration, overwhelm, disconnection, dysfunction, and drama?

CASCADING RITUALS

Craft rituals that will create the greatest ripple effect in your life. Some rituals, while important, will have a relatively small impact on the rest of your life. We're looking for rituals that, once established for an extended period of time, make other changes easier.

Let's look at a morning ritual that has become popular for good reason. Green smoothies. Drinking green smoothies sets in motion a series of effects that contribute to positive changes in other areas of life.

Let's say your soul desires to feel vibrant, alive, and energetic. You, wisely, commit to adding a green smoothie to your morning ritual once a week. When first integrating a ritual, start with a small change. Cultivating and ingraining one small part of your ritual is more important than tackling a complex ritual right away.

Here's how it might look.

When you're at the market on Sunday, you pick up a few extra apples, cucumbers and kale leaves. When you get home from the market, you pull out your blender and pop it in front of your coffee maker, and you put an apple on the top of the blender to remind yourself it's smoothie time.

When you wake up on Monday morning and head to the kitchen, your blender is a visual reminder of your smoothie commitment. You pull out your delicious produce and pop it in your blender. Down goes the smoothie. We want to start with a small and simple, soulful change. Yes, you could launch into a five-day smoothie cleanse, but that kind of change is usually not sustainable.

After a few weeks of your Monday morning smoothie ritual, you'll start to notice how automatic your soulful change has become. A funny thing happens as time passes. At the market, it's easy to add more apples, cucumbers and kale leaves into your bag. Tuesday morning arrives and you put your produce in the blender without even thinking about it. Slowly and surely you begin to expand your green smoothie ritual into the rest of your week.

The days pass and months unfold and the soulful change of adding green smoothies into your life becomes easier. Your green routine becomes more automatic and the repetition begins to build a state of automatic ease. Your ritual is ingrained.

You start to feel more vibrant, energetic, and alive. Your mind becomes clearer and your body feels lighter. The overall increase in wellbeing gives you the psychological boost you need in order to reduce emotional eating. You'll start to notice how much better you feel when you start your day off with living food, and you'll wonder how else you might be able to improve your life. Soon you'll pull out your annual soul plan and pick something else to craft a ritual around.

Your commitment to one green smoothie per week streams into a cascade of soulful changes that supports you in living a life you love.

When creating rituals, start by identifying which of your intentions requires a ritual in order to be achieved. Next, break down what you want the entire ritual to look like. For example, a complete ritual might look like this:

Intention
I intend to nurture my desire to feel vibrant, energetic and alive by adding more whole, living, and green foods into my life.

Actions
- Buy a fancy blender
- Find a green smoothie recipe I love
- Add more green stuff into my weekly grocery shop
- Make myself a green smoothie every Monday morning

Ritual
Sunday
- buy produce at the grocery store or farmer's market
- wash and prep produce

Monday
- wake up
- make a green smoothie

Identify a small change that will move you closer to the full ritual you want to integrate. Small changes support and sustain the other significant changes you need to make in order to consistently perform your ritual. Once you have successfully made one part of your ritual automatic, you can add another part.

Go back into your annual soul plan and find an intention that you could achieve by creating a ritual.

LIFE DESIGN PROCESS – CHOOSE AN INTENTION TO SUPPORT WITH A RITUAL

My Soulful intention:

232

CUE

Next, find a cue for your ritual. In the green smoothie example, the cue could be waking up Monday morning, going downstairs, and seeing your blender sitting in front of your coffee maker. A cue can be anything – images, emotions, sounds, a TV commercial, a person, a time of day, a certain place, thoughts.

Your new ritual will initially require mental exertion. By creating a cue, you make it easier for your brain to remember what to do and move toward the change. It is extremely important to choose a ritual cue that occurs before you are automatically cued into a different, less soulful, ritual.

Ritual cues drop our level of consciousness, which is why it's important to develop a new, soulful ritual that interrupts a competing, old ritual. Let's pretend you'd like to start your day with a morning walk. The fresh air helps to clear your mind and the time in nature grounds your soul. If you wake up and immediately see your running shoes, you're more likely to put on your shoes and head out the door. However, if your iPhone is the first thing you see after waking up, you're more likely to open your email and get lost in the interwebs. Before you know it, your morning walk time has been devoured by mindless surfing and you're already feeling overwhelmed by the demands of your inbox.

Select a cue that will remind you of the ritual you want to engage in.

The cue I will use is:

RITUAL

The ritual is the behavior you want to engage in. In the example above, the ritual is the process of making your smoothie and drinking it.

Design a ritual that will allow your soulful goal to become reality: drinking a green smoothie once a week, going for a five-mile run on Sundays, making plans to hang out with your community once a month, taking a selfie and posting it to Instagram every day, and donating $10 to a charity once a week are all examples of rituals.

Keep your ritual simple by narrowing it down to three actions. If your ritual requires a more complex series of behaviors, start with three and then add more once the ritual has been established.

Craft a ritual that will support your intention.

My ritual will be:

1. ______________________________

2. ______________________________

3. ______________________________

REWARD

Finally, the reward part of the ritual is extremely important. The reward triggers your brain to decide whether or not to make your ritual permanent. The reward of drinking a green smoothie is feeling nourished, vibrant, energetic, and alive.

Your reward may be inherent within the ritual. Going for a run releases a surge of feel-good hormones. Downing a green smoothie quickly increases your level of energy and clarity. Taking a selfie and posting it to Instagram might give you a sense of connection as your community likes and comments on your beautiful face.

If your ritual is not inherently rewarding, it's important to establish a reward at the end of your ritual. For example, when I was writing this book, there were times I wanted to abandon my writing ritual. Most of the time, writing is inherently rewarding for me. However, when my frustration levels increased (typical writer's angst), my satisfaction levels decreased, and my rituals became more difficult to stick to. In order to maintain my writing ritual, I decided to tack a reward onto the end of my ritual. After I wrote for two hours, I would give myself a piece of raw dark chocolate. I would lean back in my fancy desk chair, place the chocolate on my tongue, let it melt, and feel the satisfaction of adding another 2,000 words to my writing project.

Identify the reward that will reinforce your ritual. It may be inherent or you may need to create it.

My reward will be:

Crafting soulful rituals is one of the most effective ways of creating change and making it stick. Once you've integrated a ritual into one area of your life, it will be easier to create rituals for other areas.

We create the lives we love primarily through our daily rituals. I often hear from my community that the life design process feels big. I know it can feel overwhelming, and one of the most effective ways of managing the overwhelm is to focus on designing one ritual at a time.

It takes effort to consciously craft and integrate rituals. But, over time, your new, soulful ritual will crowd out the old, unwanted rituals. Before you know it, you will be living a life you love.

PART THREE

LIVE

Even when you think you have your life all mapped out, things happen that shape your destiny in ways you might never have imagined.

DEEPAK CHOPRA

CHAPTER THIRTEEN

REALLY, WE'RE REDESIGNING

It is good to have an end to journey towards; but it is the journey that matters, in the end.

URSULA K LE GUIN

THE DESIGN OF YOUR LIFE IS REALLY A REDESIGN. IT'S SOMETHING YOU review and revise throughout the year. It is imperative to regularly take time to listen to the call of your soul and savor the process of designing your life the way you want it to be.

Your life design gets to change because you change. This is your plan to live your life on your own terms, according to what matters to you. It's a sketch landscape of the world you want to live in. Living a life you love means engaging in an ongoing process of reflecting, redesigning and rebuilding.

* * *

Pace and Kyeli began to experience moments in their relationship where they felt out of alignment. The thought, *I didn't sign up for this,* crossed their minds many times. They set a soulful relationship goal for themselves by consciously choosing to get married. Again. Pace and Kyeli have been married four times. By getting married again, they recognize the truth that people change. They are choosing to commit to the other person who, in many important ways, is not the same as when they first committed to the relationship.

Getting remarried helps Pace and Kyeli actively and lovingly devote themselves to each other, which is the perfect antidote to bitterness and resentment. It helps them get clear about what they want for themselves and the relationship. By recognizing their commitment in a sacred ceremony, they are more able to keep their hearts and souls aligned.

As I was writing this book, my true self called me into another major life redesign. I was filled with angst and hesitation. After all, I had a book to write! There were times I desperately wanted to ignore it, and, for a while I did. One evening, I lay on the earth, I opened my heart to the natural world, and welcomed its support. Smelling the sweet grass and feeling the glow of the moon on my skin, I entered into a place of knowing. After listening to the chatter in my mind, it was time to return to the home of my soul.

I felt afraid. If I walked the path of the true self, would I lose everything I had gained along the way? I felt angry. Why did I choose a life of constant evolution? Why couldn't I settle? I had a good life by conventional standards – a successful career, a beautiful home, a devoted husband, two precious children, a circle of incredible friends. Why couldn't I feel satisfied with all that was good? Why must my soul call me into another life when I was just starting to feel settled in this one? Throughout all my internal debate and turmoil, the soulful whisper was persistent: *follow your truth.*

I redesigned.

REFINEMENT

Your soul isn't static and your life shouldn't be either. Throughout the year you can look at the places in your life that need revisions, refinement, and renovation. You have the power to put your constructed self in the role of worker and let your soul be the foreman.

Creating the blueprint and designing your great life will be frustrating. At times, you may rip out entire pages and watch with satisfaction as they burn. You will pray for breakthroughs. Wait for them, they will come.

Life design is a process that allows you to be inspired by the end result while living in, and loving, the present moment. Really, you and I both know we never arrive. Life is always in process. We must always redesign. The process of designing your life creates space for quantum leaps and lights the way for baby steps. Both are essential to living a life you love.

The more I live according to the call of my soul, the more my life is packed with dreams turned reality, doors swung wide open, and green lights all the way. I travel to beautiful places, speak at wholehearted events, luxuriate in quality times with my boys, write books I want to write, feel deeply connected to my community, and get to do work I love.

Dreams really do come true, but it wasn't always this way. In the not so distant past, I felt like I was frantically chasing dreams and agonizing about achieving my goals. Looking back, I can clearly see the problem. I wasn't dreaming my dream – I was dreaming the dream I 'thought' I should have. My goal setting was unconscious, egoic, supersized, and unhealthy – and goals should only be supersized if they are soulful. Supersizing egoic goals can be disastrous and devastating.

Living in the truth of an authentic goal feels good. Nourishing. Inspiring. Energizing. When I first began designing my life, I neglected to redesign. I tossed the dream of my life into the future and kept walking towards it no matter what. Life is rarely a straight line. We are meant to curve, evolve, adapt, and change our minds. Dream refinement is a necessity. We must redesign.

Get out your calendar and block off at least three chunks of time to sit down and consciously engage with your life design.

How is it going? What needs to be refreshed? Has your truth changed? What needs to be added? What needs to be dropped?

If the design of your life feels heavy, obligatory, or stagnant, play with these journal questions to help you refine your dreams and redesign your soulful goals.

Why do I want the goal I think I want?

Whose dream is this?

How do I feel about stepping in the direction of this goal?

What does an authentic goal feel like?

How can I refine the design of my life even more?

WHEN THE GOING GETS TOUGH

All the hurts and failures, all the wanderings, losings, dyings, and forgettings were but part of the gaining of the rich material of your life. By being wounded, you become vulnerable and available; by being lost, you were able to be found; by dying, you learned the power of new birth; by forgetting, you gained the joy of remembering.

JEAN HOUSTON

Once you have completed your life design, you may feel a massive desire to express yourself and step into your big, meaningful life. Moments later you may feel overwhelmed, idealistic or think, *yes, but...* You may feel hungry to make a difference in the world, but feel scared when you think about how.

In an attempt to avoid the complicated questions, you may put your life design on the shelf. Days, months or weeks later you may find yourself bored, unfulfilled, critical, feeling blah, cynical, and wondering how your life got so off track. These messages are from your true self – it is trying to make you uncomfortable so you can remember the call of your soul.

Designing and living a life you love does not mean your life is without pain. When the going gets tough, it's important to be conscious of the purpose in the pain. Injury, trauma, rejection, loss, betrayal, broken hearts, and failure are all part of the cosmic dance of life.

Stay with it. When we try to run away from the pain of life, we slip back into old patterns and unhealthy coping mechanisms. If we run, we enter into a cycle that feeds more unhappiness, life avoidance, and disappointment. Ultimately, the more we try to avoid the pain of being human, the further we drift from the life we love.

Life is conspiring to support us. It is a benevolent force that is always guiding us toward a great life: an unexpected illness illuminates what deeply matters, you bump into your soul mate on the day of your engagement, a job you were waiting for falls through and you are forced to see a more truthful opportunity, a friend calls to share a tragic story that relates directly to the dilemma you are facing, a random Facebook post gives you the answer you were searching for.

Trust life.

DARK NIGHT OF THE SOUL

When committing to the sacred adventure of designing your life, you may experience a dark night of the soul. A dark night of the soul shatters the identity of the constructed self. The masks we once wore can no longer be worn. Everything falls away.

Experiencing the dark night is natural. It's a universal phenomenon that spans the ages. Feeling abandoned, lonely, and isolated is common when you are in a dark night. Solitude will be your companion. The dark night is indeed without light, but it is not without love. It's an unavoidable calling into the soul. You will hear whisperings of truth and authenticity if you listen closely.

The soul is both creative and destructive. Within the dark night, destructive forces are unleashed and all that is false about your life will be hacked away. Fragile beliefs shatter. What we thought we knew is burned to a crisp. Purpose fades away. Necessary destruction makes space for truthful creation.

When designing your life, it is difficult to move into what is true without destroying what is false. A dark night will serve your life. When you find yourself in a dark night, your tools will be contemplation, intuition, discernment, mindfulness, and trust. They will serve you well if you let them.

After a dark night, we can no longer return to what was; we can only move into what will be. Although a dark night is uncomfortable and undesirable, keep moving through it. Numbing and distracting will only get you into trouble. Create new beliefs. Transform your identity. Deepen your awareness. Learn your internal rhythms. Define your life on your own terms.

To be free, we must be willing to go where we are most afraid to go. We must be willing to lose what is comfortable and familiar and edge into the darkness and the unknown. There is wisdom in the darkness. Remember, the light will always return.

When you are in the dark moments, slow the pace of your life so you can tend to your heart and listen to your soul. Open space so you can discern between darkness and drama. Opt out of drama. Make space for darkness.

* * *

Kyra Bussanich was diagnosed with an autoimmune disorder when she was 20 years old. For years, she experienced debilitating chronic pain and underwent numerous medical procedures. She was working at a job she didn't enjoy and her husband asked, "If you could do anything you wanted, what would it be?" She answered: "go to pastry school." Kyra listened to her true self. She quit her job and enrolled in the prestigious Le Cordon Bleu patisserie program.

The journey wasn't always easy for Kyra. In fact, sometimes it was terrifying and required significant sacrifice. Now, Kyra's body is thriving and so is her soul. She is a three-time winner of the Food Network show *Cupcake Wars* and she creates beautiful and delicious gluten-free treats at Kyra's Bake Shop in Lake Oswego, Oregon. When Kyra looks back at her dark night of the soul she says, "I absolutely know there was purpose in that pain. If I didn't go through it, I wouldn't be doing what I am doing today. I love the life I am living now."

* * *

When we summon the energy, strength, courage, and resolve to sacrifice what depletes us and affirm what nourishes us, we thrive. It may cost you your job, your belief system, your home, or your relationship. The cost of the sacrifice ends up being far less than the cost of ignoring a lifetime of ache and hunger. It may cost you everything and you may find everything.

Designing a life you love doesn't mean life is always rosy; it means you have the courage to adventure into the rich jungle of your most authentic life, knowing you might stumble into darkness from time to time.

SELF-LOVE

If you find yourself in a tough spot while designing a life you love, examine your relationship with yourself. Your outer world is a reflection of your inner world.

Your relationship with yourself influences what you eat, how much you exercise, the relationships you welcome into your life, how you handle money, the career you choose, the boundaries you set (or don't), your creativity, how you parent, the habits you develop, the thoughts you think, and the emotions you feel.

Is your relationship with yourself based on love or fear? Fear will push you to strive for success, recognition, and approval in an effort to avoid rejection or disappointment. You connect to fear when you belittle yourself, criticize yourself, shrink, hide, dim your light, defend yourself, respond with cynicism, toss out sarcasm, and attack yourself or others.

On the other hand, love calls on courage and authenticity to help you show up in your life in a truthful and meaningful way. You connect to love when you speak your truth, listen to your soul, nurture your body, attend to your mind, establish loving boundaries, live wholeheartedly, take time for yourself, and do what deeply matters.

If you feel like love is a long way off, you can locate it by asking, *how would I act right now if my relationship with myself was based on love?* Make a commitment to follow through with the answers that emerge.

The more you love yourself, the easier it is to live a life you love. However, even if you love yourself unconditionally, you will still encounter times of stress. When we are stressed, our conscious control becomes tired, and our stale patterns are more likely to be activated. In these moments we are most vulnerable to regressing into self-sabotage.

There are still times when I sabotage myself and get caught up in the frenzy of life – fixing, planning, numbing, projecting, sacrificing, and compromising. I let my constructed self take the lead and I fall into old patterns. During these phases I hardly recognize myself when I look in the mirror. My eyes lose their spark. My body aches. My essence is dim. I spend weeks in a state of limbo knowing I've lost my connection to my true self by neglecting self-love.

This pattern surfaced one day at the farmer's market. I was eating a piece of Princess Cake after a disappointing morning. I was on the verge of tears and trying to numb the sadness with sugar and distract myself by writing. Thankfully, because I've been in this place many times before, I recognized it for what it was. I had allowed my constructed self to take the lead and my true self was neglected. Even though I was working on living my great life, living with intention, and taking action on my soul plan, fear was in control.

I checked myself: caffeine-induced anxiety, everything on my task list felt urgent, and my mind was foggy because I had neglected my meditation practice. I allowed my dreams for the future to interrupt the love I had for myself in the present. It was time to redesign and find my way home.

SABOTAGING SELF-LOVE

Knowing these unhealthy patterns and recognizing them when they show up is critical. Are you the cooperative and compliant nice guy or girl? Are you the ambitious achiever who, as soon as one goal is attained, quickly moves on to another because you still feel empty? Are you hiding in a safe, small, secure world and you feel like there's something missing? When you feel powerless, do you scramble to regain control by obsessing over your environment or trying to control others?

I'm not knocking the strategies we revert to. At some point in our lives, they served a purpose. When you find yourself in the middle of an unhealthy pattern, it's helpful to reflect on whether or not you will continue to sacrifice yourself and your life to the automatic responses.

Typically, these responses are born from past trauma – from a small child who felt defenseless and unable to cope. We developed these powerful patterns to help us survive. History was what it was. In order to create new patterns and find freedom in the present, it's important to acknowledge the purpose of the past pattern.

If we feel overwhelmed by life as an adult, or felt powerless as a child, three reflexive responses typically surface.

1. We avoid what seems overwhelming. This can show up as denying, procrastinating, repressing, running, and dissociating.

2. We control what seems overwhelming. This can show up as manipulation, abuse of others, seeking out positions of authority, status-seeking, and passive-aggressive behavior.

3. We submit to what seems overwhelming. This can show up as accommodation, self-sacrifice, self-sabotage, wishy-washy decision-making, lack of personal boundaries, loss of personal integrity, feelings of disempowerment, codependency, and being 'nice' by being compliant.

When we are aware of these three reflexive response categories, we are more easily able to catch them when they occur and choose a conscious response.

The pattern I engage in that causes me to sabotage myself is ...

The purpose this pattern served in the past was ...

Instead of engaging in my reflexive pattern, I will ...

If you feel a reflexive response trying to emerge, stop, breathe and give yourself space to craft a response that is based on the desire of your true self and not the conditioning of your constructed self.

We all have parts of ourselves that make us feel uncomfortable. It may be temping to ignore fears, mash down insecurities, and shovel anxieties into a black hole. I've learned the hard way that avoiding the darker aspects of who I am is a recipe for disaster. As they say, what we resist persists.

When we avoid the uncomfortable stuff, or try to numb it away, it doesn't go away. The uncomfortable pops up in unconscious ways and makes a mess of the life you love. When the going gets tough, it's natural to repress truth, deflect responsibility, numb the scary things, and protect your constructed self. Don't. Instead, have a conversation with yourself. It may not be a comfortable conversation, but it is worth the self-discovery. You may see what needs to be seen in order to be who you really are.

Whether you are in a dark night of the soul or in a difficult time, seek out support from a loved one or a trained professional. When you resist the urge to repress and deflect, you will emerge as a more complex and accurate version of yourself. Once you have navigated through the difficult times, you will feel stronger exploring the realm of fear and committing to the design of your life, despite the challenges.

UNCONSCIOUS FEAR

When the going gets tough, sometimes it's because unconscious fears are arising. Most of us are governed, to some extent, by unconscious fears. When fear peeks into consciousness, it's an opportunity to dive into the two primary and messy fears we struggle with as humans: fear of overwhelm and the fear of abandonment.

Fear of overwhelm emerges from feeling small in a world that is big and powerful. From this we develop coping strategies, like over-accommodating the needs, desires, and wills of others. We avoid the challenges of life and we become passive.

Fear of abandonment emerges from feeling like we were not treated with tenderness and care. From this we develop coping strategies like trying to control others, avoiding intimacy, sidestepping vulnerable situations, searching for reassurance, trying to create connection with force, and developing patterns of co-dependency.

Of all the difficulties we face as we adventure through life, the greatest will be the ones we place in our own way when we do not look at what needs to be examined.

As you are designing a life you love, you will encounter moments of pain and fear that cause you to pause. This isn't a regression, it's an opportunity to rest, reflect consciously, and gather your courage. Two steps forward and one step back is still designing a life you love. The adventure of living a great life is a journey of taking one step closer to who you really are. Repeatedly.

If I could be in this space of pain without trying to make it go away I would ...

I intend to stay present to the ache of this loss by ....

If I let this difficult time open me, I would ......

What is fear trying to protect me from?

What did I say yes to that my soul wanted to say no to?

When exactly did I lose myself?

What do I need to remember in order to find my way back to the life I love?

What are the gifts hiding in the darkness?

REFLECTION

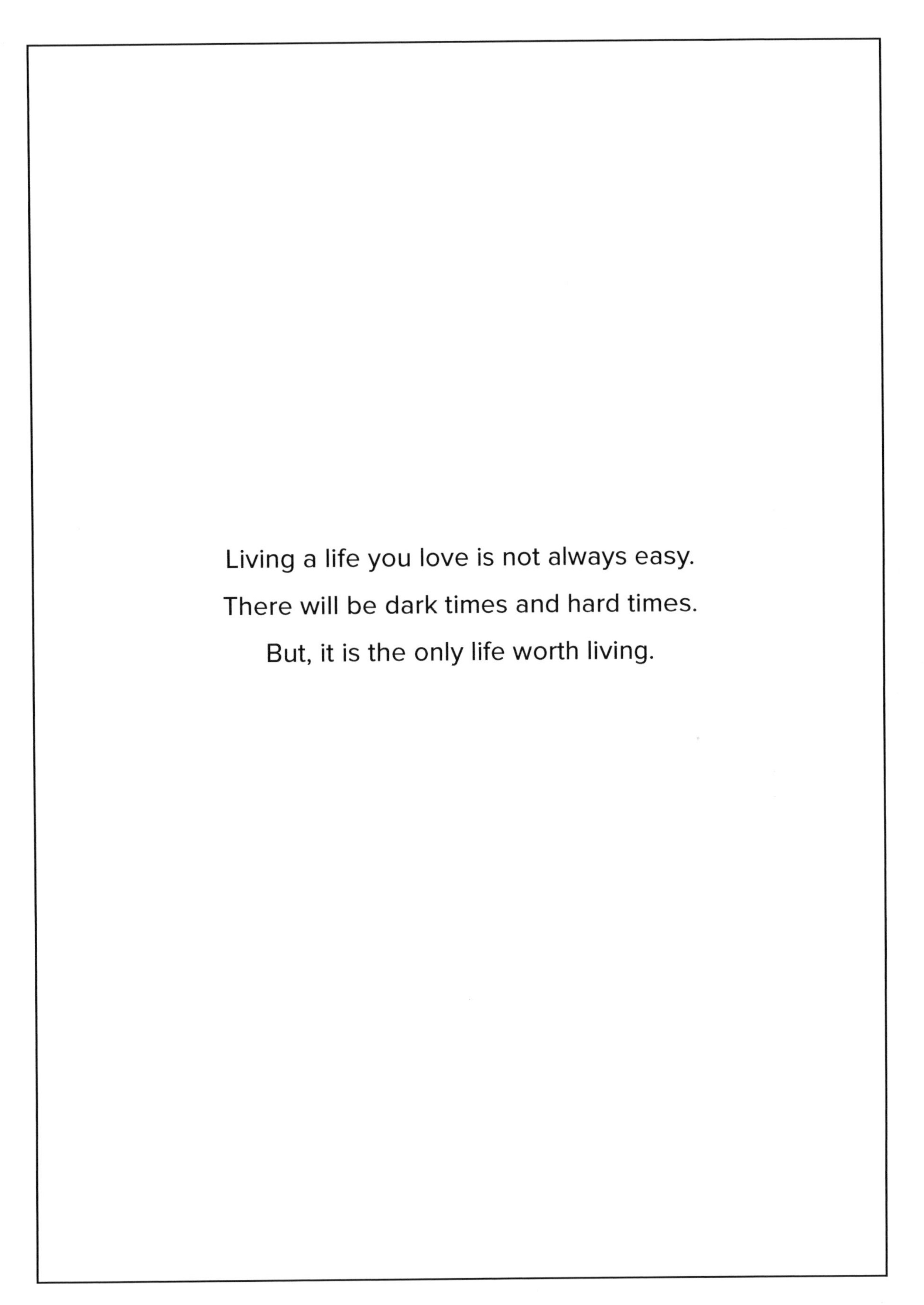

Living a life you love is not always easy.

There will be dark times and hard times.

But, it is the only life worth living.

CHAPTER FOURTEEN

COURAGEOUS COMMUNICATION

And the day came when the risk it took to remain tight in a bud was more painful than the risk it took to blossom.

ANAÏS NIN

COURAGEOUS COMMUNICATION IS ABOUT EXPRESSING YOURSELF OPENLY and truthfully without defensiveness or blame. You're going to have to converse with others about the design of your life. Entering into these conversations with the intention of honest expression, authenticity, integrity, self-awareness, compassion, and thoughtful vulnerability is the essence of courageous communication.

Authenticity is based on self-awareness and self-acceptance. While there is no right or wrong way to express your true self, here are a few suggestions.

Keep it real. It can be easy to divert into more comfortable territory when facing a potentially stressful conversation, but by keeping it real and returning to the heart of what matters, you create the right conditions for meaningful connection.

Be present. Act as though this conversation is the most important conversation you will ever have. Because, in the moment, it is.

Trust your true self. Your constructed self is going to try to wiggle in and pull you into old patterns. If you notice yourself slipping into shame, blame, guilt, fear, defensiveness, sarcasm, or future-tripping, take a break. Reconnect with your true self, reflect on your intentions for the conversation, and try again.

Breathe. Take your time. Pace yourself. You don't have to figure everything out in one conversation. Speak your truth and be willing to let it float in silence if necessary. You don't have to justify or explain yourself, unless you want to. Insight and understanding can evolve when we allow space between our words.

Be open. Keeping your questions open allows for expansion. A question like, *I'd love to hear what you think about* ... is more conducive to openness than, *do you believe in ...?*

Invite curiosity. When we enter into conversation with curiosity, we allow ourselves to see things differently and to be surprised by what we discover. Try starting the conversation off by saying, *I'm really curious about* ... instead of *why would you ...?*

What conversation are you avoiding? Why?

What are you most afraid of?

What do you most want them to know?

When you have this conversation, what will be your intention?

KNOW YOUR BOUNDARIES

> Anything or anyone that does not bring you alive is too small for you.
>
> **DAVID WHYTE**

Your boundaries are an invisible rulebook that guides your interactions with others. They define how you communicate, what you give, what you receive, how you allow yourself to be treated, and how you treat others.

Your boundaries are often a reflection of how much you love yourself, how much you respect yourself, and what you value.

When your boundaries are porous, your energy leaks out and you have less mojo to design a life you love. People who do not know their boundaries are often either doormats or bulldozers. When we allow people to walk all over us and we slip into self-sacrificing, people-pleasing, becoming a martyr, playing the victim, or sliding into self-righteousness, we have doormat boundaries.

On the other hand, a person with bulldozer boundaries will smash through others' boundaries, have rigid rules, and a strong sense of entitlement. Bulldozers often win during times of conflict, but lose respect, safety, and intimacy within the relationship.

We live courageously, consciously, and can deepen our sense of community when we have healthy boundaries. Ultimately, the more we know and honor our boundaries, the more we can show up as the friend, partner, and parent we want to be.

Here's the most important thing to remember about establishing healthy boundaries: once you have set your boundaries, release your attachment to the outcome. We must let go of what we can't control. If we are trying to control the outcome or the other person, we slip into manipulation, which feels awful for everyone. Be clear about what happens if the other person is unable to respect your boundaries. It's important to do what you need to do in order to compassionately protect your boundaries, but it is not up to you to control the other person, make them see it your way, or force them to behave a certain way.

If you feel resentment within a relationship, it's a strong signal that your boundaries may need refinement. If you are acting from a sense of duty, demand, obligation, or begrudging commitment, your boundaries need to be examined. Half-hearted living won't feel good to you and ultimately does a disservice to your relationships.

Self-sabotage, over-commitment, and co-dependency are all signs that your boundaries need a little loving attention. I call this attention your sacred yes and your honoring no.

SACRED YES

A sacred yes is a yes that honors your soul. It's a deep, authentic, full-body yes. A sacred yes may feel challenging, but it will also feel liberating. A sacred yes won't be wrapped up in the battles of your constructed self: *if I don't say yes I'll be rejected or I might miss out, so I'm going to say yes.* A sacred yes is a willing surrender to what your soul desires most.

Knowing your sacred yes means noticing when you have a twinkle in your eye or when you feel a surge of enthusiasm running through your veins as you think about moving in a particular direction. It's about noticing the moments when you have a skip in your step because you feel light and free. Paying attention to the ideas you think about over and over with real excitement means you are noticing your sacred yes.

Embracing your sacred yes means allowing yourself to rest in the sweet spot of saying yes to designing a life you love. It's a space where you welcome soulful ideas, authentic conversations, and truthful expression. When you answer yes to the desires of your heart and the longing in your soul, you are living your sacred yes. It means daring to satisfy the cravings of your true self, whether it's splashing paint on a canvas, opening a spa, starting a non-profit, reading a book, being a stay-at-home parent, climbing the corporate ladder, cuddling in bed all day, or traveling the world.

When I approached the life design tribe about what their sacred yes moved them toward, they responded enthusiastically. Sacred yes inspired them to:

> Start a non-profit, take a photography course, forgive my father, learn how to make green juice, make my meditation practice a priority, spend more time in nature, speak my truth to my spouse, embrace my Shadow, drive to the mountains once a week, learn aerial yoga, volunteer in a meaningful way, listen to educational audio books on my drive to work instead of the irritating and depressing news, be present in my body, be

unconditionally willing to feel or experience whatever is present, schedule 'do nothing' time and stick to it, masturbate, make time to read the Garfield comic and Dear Abby column every day, adorn my home, learn guitar, buy myself fresh flowers, sprinkle fresh herbs in my scrambled eggs, walk, dance, take naps, create a sacred space for myself with an altar I love, journal to remind myself of all the good things I bring to the world, breakfast in my garden, light candles at dinner, give away my clothes that don't fit, sail, write, go to the movies by myself, soak in Epsom salts, spray lavender essential oil on my bed sheets, write a book.

Your sacred yes means you refuse to be silenced, held back, dimmed, or diminished. Your sacred yes is what allows you to claim your true self, step into your authentic potential, and design a life you love.

In other words, your sacred yes is really, really, really important.

What are your signs of a sacred yes?

Three sacred-yes commitments I will make this year are ...

1. ____

2. ____

3. ____

HONORING NO

There are heaps of ideas, goals, lists, roles, and demands pulling at our attention. In order to move life design from a concept into reality, we need clear boundaries, spaciousness to make conscious choices, and laser-beam focus. We must set and respect boundaries for ourselves and for others.

Your honoring no is your boundary. Say what you mean, mean what you say, call on the courage to speak the truth, even if your voice shakes. Your honoring no will support you in being kinder, more genuine, and more real – to yourself and to others. You may say no more often, but as a result, you are freer to say yes when it works for your heart and your great life.

An honoring no is not a rebellion or a harsh refusal; it's a way of saying no that honors your true self, the other person, and your relationship. It's kind and clear. An honoring no establishes boundaries that protect your soul and the life you love.

* * *

Before designing her life, Noelle was a self-described people-pleaser. She would over-extend herself, say yes when she wanted to say no, and try to be everything to everyone. Her husband traveled for work, so she was a full-time mom to three kids, the president of the playschool, she worked as a travel agent, and taught fitness classes. She was constantly on the go, trying to juggle both her professional commitments and her children's academic and extra-curricular commitments.

One particularly challenging spring morning, she was trying to coax her tired and fighting children into the car so she could shuttle them off to school. In the chaos of the moment, she was able to lean into her sacred yes and honoring no and connect with what mattered. "We're not going to school today," she declared. Her soul knew her family needed a break, so she listened to the call and spent the entire day at a park.

After the day in the park, Noelle redesigned her family's schedule. Rather than being jam-packed with commitments and to-do lists, she added spaciousness and freedom. "With the soulful schedule, the kids are happier and I'm happier," says Noelle. Her awareness as a mother shifted after she designed her life. In the past, she was focused on the conventional role of being a parent. Post-life design, she is committed to inspiring her kids by modeling how to live a great life. When asked what she would suggest for other people who are finding their sacred yes and honoring no, she says: "Don't wait for the breaking point to do these kinds of things – even if it means missing a day of school or skipping a commitment. Say no when you need to. Say yes to what matters."

What are your signs of an honoring no? In order to honor my true self I will stop ...

I will extricate myself from what is dimming my light by ...

Three honoring no commitments I will make to myself this year are ...

1. ______________________________

2. ______________________________

3. ______________________________

WHEN YES BECOMES NO

As you are designing a life you love, there will be times when your sacred yes becomes an honoring no. If you value integrity, changing your mind may feel edgy for you. You are not alone.

My wise mentor, Larry, taught me a valuable lesson about integrity. Here's the quickie version of the story. Larry and I had been meeting for five years. We would meet in a coffee shop and talk about life, love, and livelihood. During one particularly challenging phase in my life, I rescheduled my weekly meeting with Larry four weeks in a row.

When we finally met, he taught me how important it is to do what you say you're going to do. It's respectful, it's necessary for trust, and it strengthens integrity. And then, he told me he was dying.

That moment seared the value of integrity into my soul, and I transformed Larry's lesson into a prison of fear. Once I made a commitment, I would stick to it no matter what.

It didn't matter if the terms changed, the relationship deteriorated, or the job made me want to drive off a bridge. Fear led me to believe that once I made the decision, said yes, or signed my name, I was committed. Forever and ever.

And then, I woke up. Integrity doesn't mean, do what you say you're going to do no matter what, which was my fearful interpretation. Integrity is about having strong moral and ethical principles.

Be honest. Speak your truth with love. Let your sacred yes transform into a honoring no if needed.

* * *

Kate Northup began an intensive workout and nutrition program to get in shape for her wedding. Her body quickly transformed and she felt awesome. She felt so great that once her three-month commitment was complete, she signed up for another three months – even though she had been feeling somewhat philosophically misaligned with the program for several weeks. It had started to feel masculine and outwardly focused, and she wanted to listen more deeply to her body.

But, Kate had signed up with her coach and paid her fees, so she kept on going, even though her true self was whispering, *it's time to be done*. Soon, the symptoms set in: irritation at the gym, complaining about her coach, growing resentment, insomnia, allergies, and constipation.

Kate could have taken a Tylenol PM, Claritin, and a laxative to repress the symptoms, but she didn't. She listened to the truth of her body and soul. She withdrew her commitment to the program and reconnected to her center. "When we've gotten off track, there are always signs," says Kate. "We may feel rushed, resentful, irritated, or exhausted all the time. We may have strange symptoms arise that we've never had before. When we choose to push through the emotional signs that we're off track, our body takes on the responsibility of delivering the message. Our emotions are guideposts. Our bodies are messengers. They'll let us know when we're off track. Then, it's our job to listen and recommit to what we truly desire." The day Kate recommitted to her truth, her body responded, and her health returned.

* * *

As you begin playing with your sacred yes and honoring no, you may feel uncomfortable. But, what's more uncomfortable is to live in fear, resentment, and pressure because you said yes when your true self wanted to say no.

CHAPTER FIFTEEN

EMBARKING

The privilege of a lifetime
is being who you are.

JOSEPH CAMPBELL

WHEN I LOOK BACK AT MY STORY AND THE STORIES OF OTHER LIFE Designers, I trust that anyone can design a life they love if they listen to the call of their soul. Even when I consider the suffering in the world, I trust there is purpose in the tremendous pain I see. I have to believe this. My trust in life is what gives me the strength to take another step, write another word, and open my heart a little more.

The life you love will always be in process. The art of tuning into your true self is the work of uncovering your natural wisdom, truth, and love. Your awakened heart and unveiled soul are always accessible to you. If it feels like you are inventing the truth of your soul or importing wisdom from someone else, please know you are actually in the process of rediscovery. You will connect with people who will support you and guide you along the way, but ultimately, you do the uncovering and the discovering on your own.

It's my job as the author to provide information and inspiration, and it's your job to decide to take the next steps. Life has given us each a precious responsibility – to live as fully, freely, and deeply as we can. To move from survive to thrive, from fear to love, from false to true. To follow our hearts and listen to the whispers of our souls. Live a life you love with all your might. Live and love with urgency, but not with haste.

Designing a life you love means entering into an intimate relationship with your true self. You know what you need and desire in order to live a life you love. You know what your soul longs for and what it craves. You know where your soul feels most at home and where it wants to belong. You know what restores your soul and what reassures it. You know what worries it and overwhelms it. You know what brings it joy and what causes it despair. By returning, repeatedly, to these life design processes, you will deepen self-awareness and strengthen your ability to design, and live, a life you love.

Your great life is a sacred adventure. It's not something you will fall into. It's a quest to listen to the call of your soul, trust it, claim the life you love, and use your life to transform the world for the better. How you transform the world is entirely up to you. You may plant a garden, write a book, take photos, raise a child, become a philanthropist, donate to your local food bank, fill a backpack with school supplies and offer it to a child in need, shovel your neighbor's sidewalk, donate your prom dress to a teenager who can't afford one, write poems for people, or sign up to host a little free library {littlefreelibrary.org}.

There is no-thing you need to do; you must do your soul-thing. Your life will be fulfilling, distinctive, and relevant because you designed it that way.

Life designers choose to bloom and flourish not because it's easy, but because it's worth it. The benefits are indisputable. When you find the path of the life you love, claim it. It is yours. The world needs you to live your true life. The time is now.

You are living a life you love for you, but you are also living it for us. The impact of how we live reverberates through the lives of everyone we encounter. Our family, friends, neighbors, co-workers, baristas, strangers on the street, and people on the other side of the world are affected by how we choose to show up. There is an invisible thread that connects us all. Every choice we make echoes through the world and tips us in the direction of more love or more fear. By living your great life you are adding to the love in the world.

GRATITUDE

My sons, you are my sun. My world will always revolve around you.

Mom, I am able to give to others because you gave so much to me. Thank you.

Bri, my first soul sister, cheerleader, sparring partner, and companion. I'm so glad we're doing this life together.

Dad, your tenacity and entrepreneurial spirit helped me see what I needed to see so I could do what I needed to do.

Matt, your steadfast devotion gave me a solid foundation to stand on while I was testing my wings. Your strength helped me to soar. I will always be grateful for you.

My Angel Twinsie, Annika Martins, I thank the divine for you. Every day.

Tremendous appreciation to my ultra talented team. Without you, what I do would be confusing, ugly, and boring. Thanks for being awesome and doing awesome.

> Cheri Hanson, editor extraordinaire. Endless thanks for generously sharing your insightful ideas, remarkable skills, and kind encouragement. Without you, this book would not be.
>
> Shauna Haider and the talented crew at We Are Branch, thank you for adding beauty and style to my words. Your savvy brings a whole lot of soul to my work and the world.
>
> Paul Jarvis, the web designer who created my beautiful Internet home. Thank you for creating a soulful place for my words to land.
>
> Amanda Farough, the web designer who created vibrant spaces for my passion project to hang out. Thank you for making me a cooler person.
>
> Clay Adams, the graphic designer who makes everything look good. I appreciate your keen eye, flexible nature, and quick turnaround.
>
> Dominique Chatterjee, the editor who organized and clarified my words when I was testing out my writing wings. Thank you.
>
> Casie Vitt and Steve Knight, my event team at the Fairmont. You gave me the inspiration to go big and add the luxe factor to my events. Sharing homemade ginger ale and talking

shop is always a highlight of my year.

Stefan Makwana, the photographer who expertly captured the expression of my soul through images. Your photos bring life to my work.

My soul sisters, you remind me of who I am and how to keep it real — Lee, Jackie, Farhana, Natasja, Andrea, Jeanne, Amber, Pat, Corrine, Phoenix, Wendy, Shannon, Sandra, Char, Crystal, Jackie, Joanne, Myrriah, Lori, Shelley, Tannis, Melsha, Melanie, Lana, Carrieanne, Whitney, Natalie, Carrie, Kari, Diane, Lindsay, Trisha, Kristen, Pace, Kyeli, Kyra, Amanda, Alexandra, Nicole, Catherine, Tanya, Tessa, Christina, Marilyn, Shannon, Rhea, Robin, Rachel, Rita, Tania, Debbie, Yavonna, Jeanie, Audra, Belinda, Sandra, Shelly, Kimberley, Beth, Nyk, Michelle, Katharina, Karen, Jill, Angela, Jennifae, Lisa, Danielle, and Jen, our sisterhood will always be sacred. I love you.

Love to the men who have been willing to dance with me in the realm of the heart, mind and soul – Sacha, Oliver, Wade, Tim, Stefan, Dave, Curt, Merlin, Michael, Craig, Mike, Chris, Robert, Robin, Mitch, and Matt.

Huge thanks to the encouragers who send me endless love through Twitter, Facebook, and Instagram. Profound gratitude for all the supporters through Indiegogo – you made this dream come true.

Love to the trailblazers, light-bringers, heroes, sheros, and mentors. I am often swept away by your steady stream of wisdom — Chris Guillebeau, Alexandra Franzen, Rumi, Jean Houston, Deva Premal, Maya Angelou, Mary Oliver, John O'Donohue, Abraham Maslow, Carl Jung, David Whyte, Marion Woodman, Mary Anne Radmacher, Mark Wolynn, Shannon Zaychuck, Jennifer Louden, Patti Digh, Chela Davison, Dave Ursillo, Danielle LaPorte, Gail Larsen, Robin Rice, Tim Francis, Ray Bard, Andrew Leonard and {of course} Larry.

To those who cracked my heart open for the good and for the bad with pain and with joy, thank you. It's the light and the dark that helped me find my way home.

Thanks to the mind-workers, body-workers, and soul-workers. Your gifts of healing, inspiration, insight, and consciousness brought me closer to liberation and love.

My clients, I cherish you and all the bits of life we have shared. Watching you design your great life has been a high honor. You inspire me.

And you. For the one who has found their way and the one who is still searching. This book is for you.

What this really means is, this book is dedicated to Love.
In all her forms.

ABOUT THE AUTHOR

Hello. I'm Gemma Stone.

On my twenty-fifth birthday while soaking in a bubble bath, sipping on champagne, and nibbling on chocolate, I started to cry.

I didn't like myself. I didn't like my life.

In that moment, I realized fear was controlling me ...

... fear of not being enough {pretty enough, skinny enough, rich enough, smart enough}
... fear of vulnerability
... fear of rejection

... fear of failure

I had built my life on a foundation of fear and I was depressed, anxious, and unfulfilled.

From that moment forward I devoted myself to living from love instead of fear and helping others do the same.

Now?

I love my life and I'm doing what I can to add love to the world.

In a world that is constantly telling you all the reasons to be afraid, I believe in finding all the reasons to love. Not in a syrupy, sweet, naïve way — in a courageous, real, vulnerable way.

Living a life you love is about living with freedom and joy, where difficult moments are more manageable, and where deep trust in yourself is found. It's about creating a soulful strategy to make your dreams and desires reality.

At the deepest level my intention is to help you live a life that is an expression of love in all ways — loving yourself, loving others, and loving the world {usually in that order}.

I'm armed with multiple degrees in psychology and a decade of experience working with thousands of people. From time to time, I take a break from my therapy chair or computer screen to rock the mic at colleges, conventions and conferences around the world.

Whether it's on the blog, in a mentorship relationship, an online group program, or at one of my live events I am here to help you live a life you love and add love to the world.

When I'm not working with my clients or flying around the world for events you can find me exploring the Rocky Mountains with my boys, meditating with my mala, or optimistically checking my mailbox for handwritten love notes.

LEGAL STUFF

I MADE REASONABLE ATTEMPTS TO ENSURE THE ACCURACY OF EVERYTHING IN this book and I strive to be responsible for my work and my life. Having said that, my legal team, AKA my lawyer friend, says I cannot assume any responsibility for errors, omissions or contrary interpretations of the information in this book. I don't assume any responsibility or liability whatsoever for what you choose to do with this information. Use your own wise judgment.

Throughout this book, I talk about various medical and mental health disorders and symptoms. There are many sources for different symptoms and I am offering one perspective. Please ensure you have the support of medical and mental health professionals when tending to your health. This book is not intended to diagnose or prescribe, but simply to offer an alternative way of seeing yourself, your health, and your life. The information in this book is not intended to provide legal, medical, mental health, accounting, or any other professional advice. The information contained herein may be subject to laws, so if you're using this material, please be responsible. While I'm a fan of bending the rules, I don't suggest you break the law.

Examples of past life design experiences are used throughout this work. They are intended to be for purpose of example only. There are no guarantees in life design. I don't claim, imply, suggest, or hint at what your outcome will be from reading this book or engaging with the life design processes. I can't know what the future has in store for you.

How your life unfolds after using the life design process will depend on your unique situation, the desire of your true self, the risks you are willing to take, the conversations you are courageous enough to have, the annual soul plan you create for yourself and, of course, the actions you take.

There are stories of life designers within this book. To respect the confidentiality of some people, names and identifying information have been changed. For other stories, the person's identity is crystal clear.

Use this book at your own risk.

Your Great Life!
a soulful and strategic guide to designing a life you love
By Gemma Stone

SUPPORT

You're not alone in the journey of designing a life you love. There's a whole world of digital support over at gemmastone.org.

Meet me in my virtual home and I'll show you around.

GEMMA STONE ON SOCIAL

f facebook.com/drgemmastone

@gemma_stone : #GreatLifeRevolution

pinterest.com/gemmastone

instagram.com/gemma_stone

Published 2015 by Gemma Stone International Inc.

Copyright © 2015 Gemma Stone International Inc.
All rights reserved.

Printed in the United States of America by Amazon.

Book design by Shauna Haider of We Are Branch
www.wearebranch.com

Interior photos by Stefan Makwana www.stefanmakwana.com

All rights reserved. No part of this book may be reproduced by and mechanical, photographic, or electronic process or in the form of a phonographic recording; nor may it be stored in a retrieval system, transmitted or otherwise be copied for public or private use – other than for "fair use" as brief quotations embodied in articles and reviews – without prior written permission from the author. Contact the author at gemma@gemmastone.org

ISBN: 978-0-9948728-0-7

51420254R00159

Made in the USA
Charleston, SC
21 January 2016